FEMINISM
A PARADIGM SHIFT

Neeru Tandon

ATLANTIC
PUBLISHERS & DISTRIBUTORS (P) LTD

ATLANTIC
PUBLISHERS & DISTRIBUTORS (P) LTD
7/22, Ansari Road, Darya Ganj, New Delhi
Tel.: +91-11-4077 5252, 2327 3880
E-mail: orders@atlanticbooks.com
Web: www.atlanticbooks.com

Published by Atlantic Publishers & Distributors (P) Ltd.

Reprinted in 2012, 2021, 2025

Printed & bound in India by Atlantic Print Services

Dedicated to

My husband Sanjay Tandon
and
my friend Sandeep Mohan
for their love and support and
for their belief in me

Preface

I spent hours, months and years concentrating upon the vision—how this study would give feminism a voice and form, and what is expected and hoped—the sound and flesh of it would do something for women in this country or elsewhere. Weighed down by the responsibilities of wifehood, motherhood, postdoctoral studies, heavy teaching loads, and social service, I tried to unearth the female psyche in literature based on the literary theories of feminism(s). After completing this work as researcher and more as a woman I do what one always does when the first sounds of life, of creation are heard, strong and distinct; I rejoice, I celebrate, I dance with my soul.

There is reason to celebrate the completion and publication of this work, for female psyche has been touched in various ways by women authors and critics who are real-life models for images in literature. I consider it a bridge we have needed to cross over on into a deeper *understanding* of and more sensitive appreciation for *women* as positive forces. There is no denying the fact, however that in spite of gender politics, a substantial body of women's writing has emerged as a result of women's literary vision. It is of great value, as it has enabled women to create and claim attention and status through writing. What I personally feel is voiced by eminent Hindi writer and a fellow of the famous Sahitya Akademi, Krishna Sobti. She says, "It feels good to know that as a woman and an individual I am my own person, and being a writer I enjoy the freedom to grow....Writing in literature has ceased to be a special category pursued largely by men only. It is also said that creative writing as a profession has been mostly the monopoly of men. Now women are also being accepted, but as a minority."

This study on the one hand dwells upon the contemporary conceptual debate, presents a critique of feminist models and marks out the definition of feminism, and at the same time gives multiple challenges to feministic issues and on the other it includes the social change discourse, the evolution and enflourishment of the concept of *understanding female* and *feminism*, women's development and its socio-cultural dimensions within its penetrability. The study, in this way, endeavours to furnish a panoramic view of the development of women debate, discern and dissect lacunae and plug loopholes in the rationality of the argument.

The central objective of this work is the theoretical investigation carried out at a somewhat abstract level and to arrive at a deeper understanding of feminist contentions. Few have dared to ask. What does it mean to be a woman? It is the nature of woman on which are founded all questions of her status and changes therein. For this understanding it is necessary to know the ideologies and movements in which a woman urges to seek her true nature and destiny, and finds contemporary expression. I am more than usually dependent on those whose work in the field has made available the data without which the present study could hardly have begun and completed. I have tried that this dependence should be duly acknowledged in the citation of sources. Having attempted to justify the methodology, it is now necessary to define the scope of the study further, by clarifying the concept of feminism. In writing about feminism, and particularly the feminist movement, the chief aim has always been to gain an understanding of the reasons for the emergence of feminism as a social movement in a certain limited number of countries. In this endeavour, I have had to apply a wide variety of methods like psycho-analytical, sociological, deconstruction and new-historicism in order to understand the female psyche and feminism in general. I draw on a generation of interdisciplinary scholarship to show that despite recurrent opposition, feminism has passed the historical test of time, largely because it has redefined itself in response to a variety of local and global politics. I attempt to place the theoretical analysis within the broader framework of world history that is essential to understand feminism. The arguments I make throughout this study respond to four basic questions:

(a) What difference does gender make? That is, how do women's experience change our understanding of social life and politics and how do women differ from each other?

(b) Why did feminist politics emerge historically and how has it changed over time and place?

(c) What do feminists want? That is, how do feminist interpretations of inequality lead to new ways of thinking and acting?

(d) Where is feminism going, and what strategies best advance gender justice?

The future of women depends on how we continue to redefine and implement feminist goals. Millions of women and their male allies are now engaged in the serious political task of transforming gender relations and gender conventions.

This study includes the major theoretical traditions along with textual studies by different authors and critics and is therefore a comprehensive study. It tells the readers about the history of feminism along with major works done in the field. Major well known feminists are put in categories according to their respective works. Various feminist theories and some terms regarding feminism are there to help the readers regarding their understanding of development in the field of Feminism. The introduction of various feminists face to face gives the feel of meeting them in person. Some topics especially Mothering, Violence against women, The New Woman, Feministy vs Mascultinity give this study a comprehensive status. I have elected to include liberal citations from the theorists and novelists themselves because I wanted to convey the flavour of their rhetoric as well as substance of their ideas, and so as to be as faithful as possible to the detail of their thoughts. I hope that it may serve as a kind of handbook for the feminist activists who wish to learn more about feminist theory, and for women and men in all walks of life, who want to know what feminism really is.

NEERU TANDON

Contents

1 The History of Feminism

The history of *Feminism* is the history of the *Feminist movement* as well as its origins. The Feminist movement emerged in around the late 19 century, with the beginnings of the first wave of feminism. Feminism, as a whole, came in three 'waves', each dealing with different aspects of the same issue; the *first wave* being the feminism movement in the 19th to early 20th centuries, which dealt mainly with the *Suffrage* movement. The *second wave* (1960s-1980s) dealt with the inequality of laws, as well as *unofficial* inqualities. The *third wave* of Feminism (1990s-current) arose from the perceived failures of the second wave.

Limiting the history of Feminism to the history of the modern Feminist Movement has been criticised by some authors as ignoring women's opposition to *patriarchy* over thousands of years. Although some find the use of the term, *feminist* prior to its coinage (sometime around 1880) "*ahistoric*", while others prefer to see "feminism" as a self-conscious and systematic ideology beginning in the late eighteenth century. The word "Feminism" appeared first in France in the 1880s, Great Britain in the 1890s, and the United States in 1910. The *Oxford English Dictionary* lists 1894 for "feminism", and 1895 for "feminist". Prior to that time "Woman's Rights" was probably the term used most commonly, hence Queen Victoria's description of this "mad, wicked folly of 'Woman's Rights'" is significant. It was the *London Daily News*, that coined the term, and by importing it from France, automatically branded it as dangerous. "What our Paris Correspondent describes as a 'Feminist' group...in the...Chamber of Deputies".

Precisely defining feminism can be challenging, but pragmatically, a broad understanding of feminism includes women acting, speaking and writing on women's issues and rights, identifying social injustice in the status quo and bringing their own unique perspective to bear on issues. Prior to the appearance of "feminist" as a label for women involved in discussing or advancing women's issues, it is not uncommon to find the term *protofeminist* used, although this defies a standardised definition as much as any other variety of feminist. Many feminist writers, and writers on feminism have yearned romantically for a Utopian and mythical past that if not strictly *matriarchal* (gynocratic), was at least *matrilineal* or at worst *equilineal*. In the 17th century, John Locke and Thomas Hobbes had observed that the maternal-child bond was a primary relationship, compared to the child's relationship to the father. French Utopian socialists of the 1830s and 1840s challenged the "natural order" stating that in the Romantic tradition, the only natural order was the mother-child bond, paternity being a legal bond defined by civil law. Women's voices are often difficult to discern in the ancient world, but classical Greek philosophers such as Aristotle and Plato sometimes claimed to be feminists (a role that is debated). Sappho might be considered a feminist by today's standards, and Lysistrata an activist. The 17th century saw the development of many non-conformist sects which allowed more say to women than the established religions, especially the Quakers. Noted feminist writers on religion and spirituality included Rachel Speght, Katherine Evans, Sarah Chevers and Margaret Fell. Next century also saw more women writers emerging, such as Anne Bradstreet, Bathsua Makin, Margaret Cavendish, Duchess of Newcastle, Lady Mary Roth, and Mary Astell, who depicted women's changing roles and made pleas for their education. However, they encountered considerable hostility, as exemplified by the experiences of Cavendish and Roth whose work was not published till the 20th century.

Astell is frequently described as the first feminist writer. However, this depiction fails to recognise the intellectual debt she owed to Schurman, Makin and other women who preceded her. She was certainly one of the earliest feminist writers in English, whose analyses are as relevant today as in her own time, and moved beyond earlier writers by instituting educational institutions for women. Astell and Behn together laid the groundwork for feminist theory in the 17th century. *The Age of Enlightenment* was characterised by secular intellectual reasoning, and a flowering of philosophical writing. The most important feminist writer of the time was Mary Wollstonecraft, often characterised as the first feminist philosopher. *A Vindication of the Rights of Woman* (1792), written in response to Gouges' "Declaration of the Rights of Women", is one of the first works that can unambiguously be called feminist, although by modern standards her comparison of women to the nobility, the elite of society, coddled, fragile, and in danger of intellectual and moral sloth, may seem dated at first, as a feminist argument. Wollstonecraft saw that it was the education and upbringing of women that created their limited expectations based on a self-image dictated by male gaze. Despite her perceived inconsistencies (Brody refers to the "Two Wollestoncrafts") reflective of problems that had no easy answers, this book remains a foundation stone of feminist thought. Wollstonecraft believed that both sexes contributed to the inequalities and took it for granted that women had considerable power over men, but that both would require education to ensure the necessary changes in social attitudes. Her legacy remains the need for women to speak out and tell their stories. Her own achievements speak to her own determination.

The *French Revolution* focused people's attention everywhere on the cry for *egalite*, and hence by extension, but in a more limited way, inequity in the treatment of women. In 1791, the *Declaration of the Rights of Man and of the Citizen* elicited an immediate response from the writer Olympe de Gouges who amended it as the *Declaration of the Rights of Woman and the Female Citizen*, arguing that if women were accountable to the law they must also be given equal responsibility under the law. She also addressed marriage as a social contract between equals and attacked women's reliance on beauty and charm, as a form of slavery.

United States

New Jersey appears to be the first jurisdiction to give the vote to women when it joined the other States to form the United States in 1776. Caroline Norton was a woman who became active in advocating rights for women, the absence of which upon entering into marriage, had become painfully aware of Feminism in America, took a slightly different course than that in Britain, and was slightly more advanced. The anti-slavery campaign of the 1830s provided a perfect cause for women to take up, identify with and learn political skills. Attempts to exclude women only fuelled their convictions further, and were instrumental in moving women like Elizabeth Cady Stanton and Lucretia Mott firmly into the feminist camp, leading to the 1848 Seneca Falls (New York) Women's Convention, where a declaration of independence for women ("A Declaration of Sentiments") was drafted. Barbara Leigh Smith describes her meeting with Mott there in her American Diary, one of many links between the movements on each side of the Atlantic. The Declaration of Sentiments became the focus for the organised women's rights movement in America. Sarah and Angelina Grimke were examples of other women who moved rapidly from the emancipation of slaves to the emancipation of women, while Sojourner Truth, a freed slave, pointed to the injustice of freeing slaves and then only giving the vote to black males. The most influential writer of the time was the colourful journalist Margaret Fuller whose *Woman in the Nineteenth Century* was published in 1845. Her dispatches from Europe for the New York Tribune also helped create a universality in the women's rights movement. Had she lived, she was expected to become the leader of the women's rights movement. Her involvement with prostitutes was the beginning of a long and at times difficult relationship between the women's movement and prostitution. Other notable feminists of this period include Lucy Stone. The interrelated themes of barriers to education and employment continued to form the backbone of feminist thought in the nineteenth century, as described, for instance by Harriet Martineau in her 1859 article "Female Industry" in the Edinburgh journal. The economy was changing but women's lot was not. Martineau, however, remained a moderate, for practical reasons, and unlike Cobbe, did not support the emerging call for the vote.

Barbara Leigh Smith and her friends started to meet regularly during the 1850s in Langham Place in London to discuss the need for women to present a united voice to achieve reform. This earned them the name of the **Ladies of Langham Place**. They included Besssie Raynes Parker and Anna Jameson. Issues they took up focused on education, employment and marital law. The Langham Place ladies again played a central role, and set up a Suffrage Committee in 1866 at a meeting at Elizabeth Garrett's home, renamed the London Society for Women's Suffrage in 1867. Soon similar committees had spread across the country, raising petitions, and worked closely with J.S. Mill. Denied outlets by establishment periodicals, women like Lydia Becker started the *Women's Suffrage Journal* in 1870. Other publications included Richard Pankhurst's *Englishwoman's Review* (1866). Tactical disputes were the biggest problem, and the membership of various groups varied over time. In France, with the fall of the conservative Louis-Philippe in 1848, feminist hopes were raised, as in 1790. Several newspapers and organizations appeared. Eugenie Niboyet (1800-1883) founded *La Voix des Femmes* (*The Women's Voice*), as the first feminist daily newspaper in France, 'a socialist and political journal, the organ of the interests of all women'. Niboyet was a Protestant woman who had adopted Saint-Simonianism, and *La Voix des Femmes* attracted other women from that movement, including the seamstress Jeanne Deroin (1805-1894) and the primary schoolteacher Pauline Roland. Unsuccessful attempts were also made to recruit Georges Sand. The enthusiasm was shortlived, feminism which was allied with socialism was seen as a threat as it had been under the previous revolution, Deroin and Roland were both arrested, tried and imprisoned in 1849.

With the emergence of a new, more conservative government in 1852, feminism would have to wait until the *Third French Republic*. Slowly but surely the protests became more vigorous, heckling, banging on doors, smashing shop windows, and eventually, by 1914, arson. In 1913, one of the group, Emily Davison, sacrificed herself on Derby Day, dying under the King's horse. These tactics produced mixed results of sympathy and alienation and many of them were imprisoned, creating an increasingly embarrassing situation for the Government.

In the nineteenth and twentieth century, the sociology of family has continued to engage feminist theorists, both in terms of debating the historical fact of matriarchy, and in its symbolism in interpreting social issues. This revolved around the theories of Bachofen and the rejection of inevitable patriarchy. This led to continuing challenges to accepted patriarchal models.

Psychoanalysis and Feminism

Psychoanalytic theory emerged during the debate on kinship, and kinship and gender relations form the core of the theoretical writings, and has been portrayed as one of the elements containing feminism. Its origins can be found in the Romantic, and in particular Bachofen's representation. The matriarchy-patriarchy conflict is central to Sigmund Freud's work, and to the schism that followed between him and Carl Jung. Freud's theories can be seen to be centred around the triangular *Oedipus complex*, the patricidal relation between child and father, and incestuous desire for the mother, as a model for the development of each individual's personality. The correspondence between Freud and Jung reveals their conflicting concepts of universal patriarchy on the former's part, and the yearning for liberation and return to matriarchy of the latter. Freud disliked feminist sexual radicalism, but echoed some of it. "*Mother-right should not be confused with gynaecocracy*". The centrality of Oedipal desire is best expressed in *Totem und Tabu* (1913). He based his anthropological speculation on the work of J.J. Atkinson, who in turn was influenced by Darwin. Freud proceeded to layer Greek myth onto the Darwinian *ethology* of the herd and the polygamous dominant male, challenged by its male offspring, a position challenged by anthropologists, but which became influential in 20th century culture. In Freudian analysis, Bachofen's world is now seen as the story of individual psychological evolution, a psychic recasting of *ontogeny mirroring phytogeny*. Woolf also started to paint homosexuality in a positive light, "*women...had almost always been seen in relation to men*", and to examine the constructs of gender more minutely. West has perhaps best been remembered for her comment: "*I myself have never been able to find out precisely what feminism is: I only know that people call me a feminist whenever I express sentiments that differentiate me from a doormat, or a prostitute.*" Women received the vote in Denmark and Iceland in 1915 (full in 1919), the USSR in 1917, Austria and Germany in 1918 (1928), and many countries including the Netherlands in 1919, Canada in 1920, and South Africa in 1930. French women did not receive the vote till 1945. Lichtenstein was one of the last countries, in 1984.

Freudian patriarchy has been blamed for the diminished profile of feminism in the interwar years, although such an implication appears simplistic, since Freudian psychoanalysis is not wholly inimitable to feminism, as Juliet Mitchell points out. The Freudian concept incorporated the original, as an image of infancy (maternal love), and he had reservations about the consequences of patriarchy.

Nevertheless, feminist scholarship did shift way from the need to establish the origins of family, as *historicism* yielded to *functionalism*, not the origins, but the process of patriarchy. Conventional academics scorned those, such as Mathilde Vaerting (1921) who wrote on matriarchy. Robert Briffault sustained a similar fate, but the theory was not quite dead, continuing to be mentioned in a variety of disciplines.

Feminist interpretation of the role of women in the wars has emphasised the preoccupation of national leaders with mobilising and regulating women. While earlier writers had depicted war as emancipating, more recent scholarship such as Francoise Thebaud and Nancy Cott emphasise the conservative effect with reinforcement of traditional imagery, and a literature directed towards motherhood. These phenomena have been called the "nationalization of women".

Despite gains over the first half of the twentieth century, the essential problems remained of discrimination, inequality and limited opportunities. In a number of countries the emergence of a new feminism after the war started to be referred to as *second-wave feminism* to reflect the hiatus the war had caused and the new directions. Later it became popular to refer to feminism prior to the war as *first-wave feminism.* However, as with much feminist nomenclature, this terminology is not uniform, for instance Lavine refers to what is described here as "Second wave", as "Third wave". He maintains that the first wave (in the United States) was the Women's Rights Movement from the Seneca Falls Convention of 1848 to the onset of the American Civil War in 1861, and the second wave, or Woman Suffrage Movement, from the founding of the National American Woman Suffrage Association in 1890 to 1924, that is, after the amendment to grant the vote was ratified. The 'Third wave' he calls the Women's Movement, and dates from 1964. One difficult issue that second wave feminism had to deal with was the increasing visibility of *lesbianism* within and without feminism. Lesbians felt sidelined by both gay liberation and women's liberation, where they were referred to as the *"Lavender Menace"*, provoking *The Woman-Identified Woman* from the Radicalesbians in 1970. Jill Johnston's *Lesbian Nation: The Feminist Solution* followed in 1973. Many lesbians felt that they should be central to the movement, representing a fundamental threat to male supremacy. In its extreme form this was expressed as the only appropriate choice for a woman. One of the more colourful lesbian feminist writers of this period was *Rita Mae Brown.* Eventually the lesbian movement was welcomed into the mainstream women's movement. The threat to male assumptions they represented turned out to be real in that their presence in the woman's movement became a target of the male backlash. One of the main fields of interest to these women was in gaining the right to contraception and birth control, which were almost universally restricted until the 1960s. With the development of the birth control pill feminists hoped to make it as available as possible. Many hoped that this would free women from the perceived burden of mothering children they did not want; they felt that control of reproduction was necessary for full economic independence from men. Access to abortion was also widely demanded, but this was much more difficult to secure because of the deep societal divisions that existed over the issue. To this day, abortion remains controversial in many parts of the world.

Many feminists also fought to change perceptions of female sexual behaviour. Since it was often considered more acceptable for men to have multiple sexual partners, many feminists encouraged women into "sexual liberation" and having sex for pleasure with multiple partners. There is a so-called *third wave*, but feminists disagree as to its necessity, its benefits, and its ideas. Often also called "Post-Feminist", it can possibly be considered to be the advancement of a female discourse in a world where the equality of women is something that can be assumed—rather than fought for international feminism.

Immediately after the war, a new international dimension was added by the formation of the United Nations. In 1946 the UN established a Commission on the Status of Women, originally as the Section on the Status of Women, Human Rights Division, Department of Social Affairs, and now part of the Economic and Social Council (ECOSOC). In 1948 the UN issued its Universal Declaration of Human Rights which protects "the equal rights of men and women", and addressed both the equality and equity issues. Since 1975 the UN has held a series of world conferences on women's issues, starting with the World Conference of the International Women's Year in Mexico city, heralding the United Nations Decade for Women (1975-1985). These have brought women together from all over the world and provided considerable opportunities for advancing women's rights, but also illustrated the deep divisions in attempting to apply principles universally, in successive conferences in Copenhagen (1980) and Nairobi

(1985). However by 1985 some convergence was appearing. These divisions amongst feminisms included: First World vs. Third World; the relationship between gender oppression and oppression based on class, race and nationality; defining core common elements of feminism vs. specific political elements; defining feminism, homosexuality, *female circumcision*, birth and population control; the gulf between researchers and the grass roots, and the extent to which political issues were women's issues. Emerging from Nairobi was a realisation that feminisim is not monolithic but constitutes the political "*expression of the concerns and interests of women from different regions, classes, nationalities, and ethnic backgrounds. There is and must be a diversity of feminisms, responsive to the different needs and concerns of women, and defined by them for themselves. This diversity builds on a common opposition to gender oppression and hierarchy which, however, is only the first step in articulating and acting upon apolitical agenda.*" The fourth conference was held in Beijing in 1995. At this conference at the *Beijing Platform for Action* was signed. This included a commitment to achieve "*gender equality* and the *empowerment of women*". The most important strategy to achieve this was considered to be "*gender mainstreaming*" which incorporates both equity and equality, that is, that both women and men should "*experience equal conditions for realising their full human rights, and have the opportunity to contribute and benefit from national, political, economic, social and cultural development.*" Now, ten years later there is still debate as to how much difference this has made.

Feminist Theory

In the immediate postwar period, Simone de Beauvoir stood alone in her fierce opposition to an image of woman in the home and in relation to men. De Beauvoir provided an *existentialist* dimension to feminism with the publication of *Le Deuxieme Sexe* (*The Second Sex*) in 1949. As the title implies, the starting point is the implicit inferiority of women, and the first question de Beauvoir asks is "what is a woman?". Woman she realises is always perceived of as "other", "*she is defined and differentiated with reference to man and not he with reference to her"*. In this book and in her essay, "*Woman: Myth & Reality"*, de Beauvoir anticipates Betty Friedan in seeking to demythologise the male concept of woman. *"A myth invented by men to confine women to their oppressed state. For women it is not a question of asserting themselves as women, but of becoming full-scale human beings."* "One is not born, but rather becomes, a woman", or as Moril Toi puts it, "a woman defines herself through the way she lives her embodied situation in the world, or in other words, through the way in which she makes something of what the world makes of her". Therefore, woman must regain subject to escape her defined role as "other", as a Cartesian point of departure. In her examination of myth, she appears as one who does not accept any special privileges for women. Ironically, feminist philosophers have had to extract de Beauvoir herself from out of the shadow of Jean-Paul Sartre to fully appreciate her. The sheer volume of critical works on de Beauvoir is a testament to her stature. While it has become fashionable in some circles to dismiss de Beauvoir as an historical artefact, others claim that all the essential elements of modern feminism can be found in her work. While more philosopher and novelist than activist, she did sign one of the Mouvement de Liberation des Femmes manifestos.

The resurgence of feminist activism in the late 1960s was accompanied by an emerging literature of what might be considered female associated issues, such as concerns for the earth and spirituality, and environmental activism. This in turn created an atmosphere conducive to reigniting the study of and debate on *matericentricity* as a rejection of *determinism*, such as by Adrienne Rich and Marilyn French while for *socialist feminists* like Evelyn Reed, patriarchy held the properties of capitalism. Critics were quick to take issue with these claims, but what really mattered was that patriarchy as right could no longer be assumed; feminists, to use Jane Ellen Harrison' phrase, had utilised the newer scientific disciplines and *"continued to lay the axe...[to] that fair family Tree"*. They had effectively returned women to history. One problem feminists have encountered in the late 20th century is a strong backlash against perceived zealotry on their part. This backlash may be due to the large amount of radical feminist activism that has been perceived as representing the feminist movement as a whole. Many women, and some men, have become reluctant to be identified as feminists for this reason. Outside of the West, feminism is often associated with Western colonialism.

2

Major Works on Feminism: A Historical Survey

15th century

- *The Book of the City of Ladies*, Christine de Pisan (ca. 1405)
- *The Treasure of the City of Ladies*, Christine de Pisan (ca. 1405)
- *The Tale of Joan of Arc*, Christine de Pisan (1429)

16th century

- *Her Protection for Women*, Jane Anger (1589)

1791

- *A Vindication of the Rights of Woman*, Mary Wollstonecraft

1861

- *Incidents in the Life of a Slave Girl*, Harriet Jacobs

1869

- *The Woman with Prospects*, Concepción Arenal (Seville, Spain)

1929

- *A Room of One's Own*, Virginia Woolf

1938

- *Three Guineas*, Virginia Woolf

1949

- *The Second Sex*, Simone de Beauvoir

1963

- *The Feminine Mystique,* Betty Friedan

1970

- *The Female Eunuch*, Germaine Greer
- *Sexual Politics,* Kate Millett
- *The Dialectic of Sex: The Case for Feminist Revolution,* Shulamith Firestone

1973

- *Beyond God the Father,* Mary Daly

1976

- *Literary Women,* Ellen Moers
- *Black Macho and the Myth of the Superwoman,* Michele Wallace
- *Of Woman Born: Motherhood as Experience and Institution,* Adrienne Rich
- *When God was a Woman,* Merlin Stone

1977

- *A Literature of their Own,* Elaine Showalter

1979

- *The Madwoman in the Attic, Sandra Gilbert* and *Susan Gubar*
- *The Bloody Chamber,* Angela Carter
- *A Literature of Their Own*, Elaine Showalter

1981

- *Ain't a Woman? Black Women and Feminism*, Bell Hooks

1982

- *In a Different Voice,* Carol Gilligan

1983

- *This Bridge Called My Back,* Gloria Anzaldúa & Cherrie Moraga

- *Women, Race, and Class,* Angela Davis
- *The Politics of Reality,* (especially "Oppression") Marilyn Frye
- *Outrageous Acts and Everyday Rebellions,* Gloria Steinem

1984

- *Pure Lust,* Mary Daly
- *Sister/Outsider,* Audre Lorde
- *Feminist Theory: From Margin to Center,* Bell Hooks

1986

- *Feminist Studies, Critical Studies,* Teresa de Lauretis
- *Blood, Bread, and Poetry: Select Prose* (1979-1985) (especially "Compulsory Heterosexuality and Lesbian Existence), Adrienne Rich

1988

- *Lesbian Ethics: Toward New Value,* Sarah Lucia Hoagland
- *Intercourse,* Andrea Dworkin

1989

- *Gender Trouble: Feminism and the Subversion of Identity (Thinking Gender),* Judith Butler

1990

- *Black Feminist Thought,* Patricia Hill Collins

1991

- *Backlash: The Undeclared War against American Women,* Susan Faludi
- *Sexual/Textual Politics,* Toril Moi
- *The Beauty Myth,* Naomi Wolf

1992

- *Revolution from Within: A Book of Self-Esteem,* Gloria Steinem

- *Women Who Run with the Wolves: Myths and Stories of the Wild Woman Archetype,* Clarissa Pinkola Estes
- *Race, Class and Gender in the U.S.*, Paula Rothenberg

1993

- *Unbearable Weight: Feminism, Western Culture, and the Body,* Susan Bordo
- *Fire with Fire: The New Female Power and How It Will Change the 21st Century,* Naomi Wolf

1994

- *Gender Outlaw,* Kate Bornstein

1995

- *Listen Up: Voices from the Next Feminist Generation,* ed. Barbara Findlen
- *To Be Real,* ed. Rebecca Walker

1997

- *The Invention of Women: Making an African Sense of Western Gender Discourses,* Oyeronke Qyewumi

1999

- *Stiffed: The Betrayal of the American Man,* Susan Faludi

2000

- *Feminism is for Everybody: Passionate Politics,* Bell Hooks
- *Manifesta: Young Women, Feminism, and the Future,* Jennifer Baumgardner and Amy Richards
- *Slut!: Growing Up Female with a Bad Reputation,* Leora Tanenbaum

2002

- *Pink Think: Becoming a Woman in Many Uneasy Lessons,* Lynn Peril

2004

- *Not My Mother's Sister: Generational Conflict and Third-Wave Feminism*, Astrid Henry

2006

- *Stripped: Inside the Lives of Exotic Dancers*, Bernadette Barton

3 The Categories of Major Feminists

Early Pioneers

- *Plato* (427-347 *B.C.E.*), Greek philosopher

Mary Wollstonecraft (1759-1797), author of *A Vindication of the Rights of Woman*

- *Mary Shelley* (1797-1851), English novelist
- *George Sand* (1804-1876), French novelist
- *Harriet Taylor Mill* (1807-1858), English thinker [3]
- *Emily Anne Eliza Shirreff* (1814-97), English activist and writer
- *Elizabeth Blackwell* (1821-1910), first female physician in the U.S.A.
- *Celia Sanchez* (1920-1980), participant in Cuban revolution and one of first women to comprise a combat squad during the revolution
- *John Stuart Mill* (1806-1873), English thinker and women's rights advocate

First-wave Feminists

- *Jane Addams* (1860-1935)
- *Rachel Foster Avery*
- *Marie Bashkirtseff*
- *Elizabeth Blackwell*
- *Sarah Grimke*
- *Angelina Emily Grimke*

- *Anna Maria Mozzoni*
- *Katti Anker Moller,* Norwegian activist on behalf of single mothers and reproductive rights
- *Clarina I.H. Nichols*
- *Sojourner Truth*
- *Harriet Tubman*
- *Virginia Woolf*
- *Frances Wright*
- *Victoria Woodhull*

Second-wave Feminists

- *Ti-Grace Atkinson*
- *Simone de Beauvoir*
- *Lorraine Bethel*
- *Susan Brownmiller*
- *Oprah Winfrey*
- *Therese Casgrain*
- *Mary Daly*
- *Angela Davis*
- *Heather Dean*
- *Carol Downer*
- *Susan Faludi*
- *Melissa Farley*
- *Shulamith Firestone*
- *Jo Freeman*
- *Marilyn French*
- *Betty Friedan*
- *Carol Gilligan*
- *Germaine Greer*
- *Carol Hanisch*
- *Kate Millett*
- *Donna Haraway*

Third-wave Feminists

- *Gloria E. Anzaldua*
- *Margaret Atwood*
- *Melissa Benn*
- *Judith Butler*
- *Lili Taylor*
- *Susie Bright*
- *Margaret Cho*
- *Ani DiFranco*
- *Corin Tucker*
- *Bell Hooks*

Radical Feminists

- *D.A. Clarke*
- *Nikki Craft,* activist from 1970 to 2006 and beyond who does not identify as second or third wave feminist
- *Andrea Dworkin*
- *Carol Keyes*

Ecofeminists

- *Carol J. Adams*
- *Helene Aylon*
- *Judi Bari*
- *Bernadette Cozart*

Dissident and Anti-feminists

- *Tammy Bruce*
- *Jean Curthoys*
- *Donna LaFramboise*
- *Camille Paglia*
- *Christina Hoff Sommers*
- *Norah Vincent*
- *Naomi Wolf*

Individualist Feminists

- *Carol Moore*
- *Sharon Presley*
- *Voltairine de Cleyre*
- *Kathy Ferguson*
- *Emma Goldman*
- *Mary Wollstonecraft*

French Feminists

- *Olympe Audouard*
- *Hubertine Auclert*
- *Marie Bashkirtseff*
- *Simone de Beauvoir*
- *Hélène Cixous*
- *Luce Irigaray*
- *Julia Kristeva*
- *Nicole-Claude Mathieu*
- *Madeleine Pelletier*
- *Pauline Roland*

NOTES

Sources

www.yahoo.com
www.writers.com
www.google.com
www.feminist.org

4 Theoretical Perspectives on Feminism

Understand female folk, studying female psyche, discovering a new identity for 'Her', telling her inner story in a truer perspective—all these statements serve as markers for several debates in feminist discussions, decide the nature of feminism and form human's studies. By women's study, I mean the academic (inter) discipline and by feminism(s) I always mean feminism in the academy, which encompasses the study of feminism (female psyche) and women's studies, as well as feminist interventions into the academy. Literature is not mere fiction, but rather is an interpretation and compilation of history, anthropology, sociology, psychology and a host of other areas. Thus, the true literary artist reveals life more accurately and with more insight than other historical facts and statistical details, because he/she deals with the truth of the human heart with the realities of man in society. In the same spirit, most of the male writers view the woman as a fallen Eve or a Mary. A few are successful in portraying the real female psyche in other fictional work. Credit really goes to female work and in fact to female authors for delineating the female psyche in the truer sense of the word.

With the advent of feminism, each and every female oriented subject has become an issue of contemporary literary debate. In literature psyche stands for soul or spirit, while psychology considers it in a larger mode. In psychology, it stands for the mind functioning as the centre of thought, emotion and behaviour and consciously or unconsciously adjusting or mediating the body's responses to the social and physical environment. To define **Feminist Psyche** is the most controversial aspect of feminist literature. Psyche contains different modes. A common trend runs through feminist group that male undermines woman's psyche by projecting her with patriarchal notions. Thus, a more meaningful subject for literary writings focuses on the idea of psychic fragmentation of the weaker sex rather than on the theme of social oppression which obviously assumes a secondary position. Psychotic rupture is perhaps the worst and the most regressive aspect of female subjectivity. The oppression of women is not only a material reality, originating in economic conditions, but also a psychological phenomenon—how man and woman perceive one-another. Feminist scholarship undertakes to de-construct the social construction of gender and all the subsidiary cultural paradigms that support it. Feminist consciousness has certainly given a fresh ardour and excitement to literary studies. A reasonably new perception of women in literature and the works by women writers have unveiled some of the prejudices at work in the traditional approaches to literature hitherto dominated by a masculine perspective. A woman's experiences of life as a member of a gender/biased society formulated her psyche. Perhaps more than anywhere else, psychoanalysis has made its biggest impact in feminist theory and gender studies. In broad terms, psychoanalysis has been adopted by feminists, not as a supplement to, or displacement of, the history of sexuality and gender studies, but as questioning them, as containing the possibility of a different way of understanding gender oppression and psyche of female folk.

Feminism has always meant independence of mind and spirit and body. Feminist effort to end patriarchal domination should be of primary concern precisely because it insists on the eradication of exploitation and oppression in the family context and in all other intimate relationships. Its theory is that men and women should be equal politically, economically and socially. It is difficult for a common man to understand female psyche in totality; so the fight was fought by feminists (especially female) to have a clear understanding and expression of female psyche. Feminism seemed to have been a vibrant political movement back in the 70s but since then it had retreated into Women's Studies Departments at colleges and universities to be studied by other academic feminists and college administrators. From the historical point of view feminism came to be perceived as simply anti-family, anti-marriage, anti-children, and perhaps even anti-religion, not to mention anti-men. Feminism presented the family as a kind of prison, with a working career on the outside as a kind of liberation. Feminism in 70s tended to portray home life as some sort of idiocy that no enlightened woman would be interested in. Meanwhile, the legal regime promoted by feminism in the West served to damage the position of housewives and mothers, with 'no fault' divorce, anti-discrimination law and 'affirmative action' to promote women. Feminist theory hates capitalism as patriarchy is often simply equated with war, racism, capitalism, feminism with pacifism, socialism, environmentalism, multiculturalism, and even vegetarianism—everything that could be considered as progressive.

Feminists of the 60s and earlier 70s attacked what they called 'sexist-ideology' and the job of feminist criticism, according to Ruthven in his *Feminist Literary Studies: An Introduction*, was 'to expose sexism in one work of literature after another' (74). Women who spoke of models of feminine behaviour were dismissed as being 'casualties of patriarchal brainwashing who have internalised the myth of female inferiority' (Ruthven 34). Feminists considered that male authored texts have obtained double standards in their treatment of male and female characters. In male authored texts women are performing only those activities by which they can keep male happy. While male has been represented as owner who distorts women by regarding them mere sexual object.

At the root of the dispute was a fundamental disagreement about the nature and psyche of women. Throughout the first wave of feminism and much of the second, there was an ongoing debate between those who believed that women and men were very similar and therefore women deserved equal treatment, and those who believed that the sexes were very different, that women were in some ways superior, and therefore women and men should be on an equal footing. The two sides are sometimes referred to as equality feminists and difference feminists. In fact, feminism could be described partly as an ongoing struggle over how to define the word woman. Again and again, feminists themselves disagreed over the issue of gender differences. This was 'the feminist divide'.

The concept of feminism pendulates from time to time and place to place. Feminism means different things to different people, ranging from a wish to change and challenge the whole existing order of things to the desire to bring about a more balanced and saner equality between the sexes and achieve a respectable individual liberty for women with their natural instincts and characteristics intact. Though equality with all its implications at various levels of society is a major issue, one of the fundamental areas where this equality matters and is desired even by the most conservative standards of feminism is in the area of marriage. The female categorization as a sex object is vehemently opposed. Women who were troubled by sexism within the family or their personal lives were attracted to feminism. The goal of feminism became for some to eliminate sexist oppression by the patriarchal society.

Feminism as movement might have originated in the West, but with the deterioration in the status of women in India and the subsequent efforts made during the freedom struggle to pave the way for equal access to education and equal status, there arose a need for feministic studies. Some of the issues evoked by the Western women were bound to be taken up by their Indian counterparts. There is a section which has lost its sense of balance while another aims at creating a woman of substance commanding respect as she executes her role with dignity, confidence and responsibility.

Postmodernism has added a new dimension to the feminist literature as well as Third World Women's problems. Third World Women are "imagined community of women with divergent histories and social locations woven together by the political threats of opposition to forms of domination (Sexist, racist and imperialist structures that are not only pervasive but also systematic".[1] The women of the Third World are portrayed as victims. The feminists who create such images, claim that they base their analysis on the shares and gendered oppression of women. In doing so, they homogenise the experiences and conditions of the Western women and apply it to women across the world.

According to the *Oxford English Dictionary*, the term 'Feminism' was first coined by the French dramatist Alexander Dumas in 1872. Since then 'feminism' has been used and interpreted in numerous shades and shapes of its meaning. The meaning of the term has been gradually transformed and now it means a 'theory of the political, economic and social equalities of the sexes.' The term combined the French word for woman, *femme*, and *isme* which referred to a social movement or political ideology. To many women this definition is inadequate. In the introduction to *The Remembered Gate: Origins of American Feminism*, Barbara Berg defines feminism as a 'broad movement embracing numerous phases of women's emancipation'. According to her, feminism gives the freedom to decide her own destiny; freedom from sex-determined role; freedom from society's oppressive restrictions, freedom to express her thoughts fully and to convert them freely to actions. Feminism demands the acceptance of women's rights to individual conscience and judgement. In general, feminism is the ideology of women's liberation since intrinsic in all its approaches is the belief that women suffer injustice because of their sex. And feminist is a woman who recognizes herself, and is recognized by others, as a feminist. That awareness depends on a woman having experienced consciousness raising, a knowledge of women's oppression, and a recognition of woman's difficulties and communalities.

Feminism basically is a critique of male dominance and of the male point of view which has forced itself upon the world. Sexual difference defines woman and causes her objectification or as the process appears in the culturalist ideology of gender. Basically, feminist consciousness posits and refers to reality, regarding women's socio-sexual existence. It is also said that outside literature the word 'feminist' was invented by a French socialist, Charles Fourier, in the early 19th century. It was used for asking franchise and was later on extended to describe a particular strand in the women's movement that stressed the uniqueness and difference for women rather than seeking equality, even to the extent of claiming superiority of women over men. Over the years, feminism has been given a range of shifting meanings and a number of movements are associated under its banner. Judith Astellara writes:

> "Feminism is a proposal for social transformation as well as a movement that strives to end the oppression of women ...... As a movement, feminism has a long history of rebellion, more or less organised but always expression, opposition to the social institutions that made possible the inferiority of women."[2]

In fact, feminism implies a vision of reality from the perspective of the women. The Third World feminists have used a definition of feminism to mean an awareness of women's oppression and exploitation within the family, at work and in society, and conscious action by women and men to change this situation. Women's agitations, which have taken the basic issues of women's subordination in family and which have challenged politics—economic system supporting the traditional status of women, constitute the core of feminist movements. In a seminar on feminist ideology held in Bangkok in 1979 (quoted in Jayawardena, 1982) feminism was defined in terms of two long-term goals:

(1) Right of women to freedom of choice and power to control their own lives in and outside home, and have control over their bodies; and

(2) Creation of more just, social and economic order naturally and internationally.

Thus, for most, feminism is an ideology which seeks not only to understand the world but to change it to the advantage of women. Though the biological distinction between male and female is an accepted fact, the notion that woman is inferior to man is no longer accepted to women in general and feminists in particular. There are some more definitions of feminism by different critics and authors.

> "Feminism must be asserted by women ..... as the basis of revolutionary social change,"[3]
>
> —Roxanne Dunbar, 1968
>
> "Feminism—A doctrine advocating the granting of the same social, political and economic rights to women as the ones granted to men; a movement to achieve these."[4]
>
> —Funk and Wagnall
>
> "Feminism is the theory of the political, economic and social equality of the sexes. It is an organised activity on behalf of women's rights and interests."[5]
>
> —*Webster Dictionary*

Thus 'feminism' is an ideological position which emphasizes the equality of gender and advocates maximization of potential of women, so that institutionally and culturally created constraints do not hinder the process and pattern of development of women. Thus, to become a feminist means to be prepared for a profound personal transformation. A feminist is one who is awakened and conscious about women's life and problem, and feminist consciousness is the experience in a certain way of certain specific contradictions in the social order. That means the feminist apprehends certain features of social reality as intolerable, as to be rejected if one is to transform the society for a better future. Some comments from famous feminist Hélèn Cixous are noteworthy:

> "For woman, writing is the passageway, the entrance, the exit, the dwelling place of the other in me—the other that I am and I am not."[6]
>
> "To be signed with a woman's name doesn't necessarily make a piece of writing feminine. It could quite well be masculine writing and conversely, the fact that a piece of writing is signed with a man's name does not in itself exclude femininity."[7]
>
> —*Castration or Decapitation?*
>
> "I shall speak about women's writing; about what it will do. Woman must write herself, must write about women and bring women to writing, from which they have been driven away as violently as from their bodies—for the

> same reasons, by the same law, with the same fatal goal. Women must put herself into the text—as into the world and into history—by her own movement."[8]
>
> —*The Laugh of the Medusa* (1975)
>
> "The future must no longer be determined by the past"—[9]
>
> —*The Laugh of the Medusa*
>
> "It is time to liberate the New woman from the Old by coming to know her—by loving her for getting by, for getting beyond the old without delay, by going out ahead of what the New woman will be."[10]
>
> "She must write herself, because this is the invention of a new insurgent writing which, when the moment of her liberation has come, will allow her to carry out the indispensable ruptures and transformations in her history."
>
> "Write yourself. Your body must be heard. It is time for woman to start scoring their feats in written and oral language."
>
> "It is impossible to define a feminine practice of writing, and this is an impossibility that will remain, for this practice can never be theorized, enclosed, coded—which doesn't mean that it doesn't exist."[11]

Generally, three basic terms require clarity in relation to their differentiated meanings. The first term is *femaleness*, the second is *femininity* and the third is *feminism*. The term 'femaleness' focuses on physical and biological differentiation between man and woman, which provides genetic variations necessary for reproduction and continuity of humanity. The term 'femininity' refers to social and cultural construction of women, wherein they are shaped differently not only in terms of representation of body but also in relation to institutionalised role-performances, internalisation of specific values and conformity to certain cultural practices. The evolutionary changes recorded through the 'Feminine, Feminist and Female' phase have either imitated man's intellectual achievements or registered protest or moved to the sphere of self-discovery. Through this quest journey, female consciousness has excavated the truth that the desire for power is very close to her heart despite perilous consequences.

Feminism is by no means a monolithic term. If one seems a common strand in a number of its varieties, it is the critique of the patriarchal modes of thinking which subordinate women to men in familiar, religious, political, economic, social, legal and artistic domains. This patriarchal ideology teaches women to internalise these concepts in the process of their socialisation. It brings into focus the concepts of gender which are man-made. Feminism broadly aims at refuting these masculinist approaches to women. It aims at bringing to focus the feminine subject matters in a distinctive feminine mode of experience. As Patricia Meyar Spacks remarks:

> "There seems to be something what we might call a woman's point of view, ... an outlook sufficiently distinct to be recognisable through the centuries."[12]

Cheri Register opines that a feminist-writing needs to fulfil one or more of the following:

> "Serve as forum for women, help to achieve cultural androgyny, provide role models, promote sisterhood and augment consciousness raising."[13]

Gynocritics as well as champions of feminism are polemic in disowning the imposition of 'femininity' on women as a social construct. Toril Moi comments:

> "Seen in this perspective, patriarchal oppression consists of imposing certain social standards of femininity on all biological women, in order precisely to make us believe that the chosen standards for 'femininity' are natural. Thus a woman who refuses to conform can be labeled both unfeminine and unnatural ... Patriarchy, in other words, wants us to believe that there is such a thing as an essence of femaleness, called femininity. Feminists, on the contrary ...insist that though women undoubtedly are female, this in no way guarantees that they will be feminine. This is equally true whether one defines femininity in the old patriarchal ways or in a new feminist way. Essentialism (the belief in a given female nature) in the end always plays into the hands of those who want women to conform to predefined patterns of femininity.[14]

Gynocriticism, ascribed to the feminist study of women's writing rediscovering women as against the modernist concepts such as uniqueness, universality and centrality, has become an ever-engrossing academic interest since the 1980s. Feminist writing and feminist criticism, however, aim at the exigency of the advocacy of the once neglected and marginalized women's voice to be pitted against phallocentrism of the received literary tradition. Dismissed of the uniqueness that tradition is in favour of installing an area of textual production that can be called 'feminine' that exists beneath the surface of masculine discourse, and only occasionally comes to the fore in the form of disruptions of 'masculine' language. Again, this basis of feminine criticism has been advanced by some radical French feminist critics such as Luce Irigaray, Hélèn Cixous and Julia Kristeva.

The stiff opposition to patriarchal authority culminates in the formulation of a characteristic feminine style. Feminism equates itself to postcolonialism and postmodernism in its awareness of the Derridan 'difference' not based on binary opposition but on differential states of multiplicity and plurality, and in its deconstruction of patriarchy. Feminism as a mode expressing woman's world view is an ongoing process in that sacrosanct male values come under attack. Women are defined in terms of the "functions they fulfill in an andocentric society; (reproduction) what separates out a particular individual from other individuals as a 'woman'? ....This separation has two aspects, 'sociological' and 'biological'. The term for the sociological function is 'woman' (Wifman), the term for the biological function is 'female' (to sucide)."[15]

Feminism surfaced in the Western world as a movement in support of the same rights and opportunities for women as for men.

By 'feminism' is meant 'both the awareness of women's position in society as one of disadvantaged or inequality compared with that of men and also a desire to remove those disadvantages. According to Alice Jardine, feminism is a movement from the point of view of, by, and for women. Sushila Singh says "The word 'feminism', however, must be understood is its broadest sense as referring to an intense awareness of identity as a women, and interest in feminine problems. Its meaning should not be restricted to the advocacy of women's rights.... The word 'feminism' has picked up so many connotations of late that it seems to have no precise meaning, and what it stands for may be easily misunderstood. According to Janet Radcliffe Richards, feminism has a strong fundamental case, is intended to mean only that there are excellent reasons for thinking that 'women suffer from systematic social injustice because of their sex', the proposition is to be regarded as constituting the essence of feminism."[16]

Feminism tends to be thought of as a movement of women, and many feminists absolutely reject the idea of allowing men into it. However, men can be as strongly opposed to the injustices from which women suffer as women can. We must accept that feminism is not concerned with a group of people it wants to benefit, but with a type of injustice it wants to eliminate. Rather than being a movement in favour of women, feminism asks people to support a movement against injustice.

Charlotte Bunch has pointed out that feminism is not about 'adding in' women's rights, but about transforming society, so that feminism may be called 'transformational politics'. Because everything affects women, every issue is women's issue, and there is a feminist perspective on every subject. Feminism is a movement which seeks, as Teresa Billington Greg wrote in 1911, "the reorganization of the world upon a basis of sex-equality in all human relations, a movement which would reject every differentiation between individuals upon the ground of sex, would abolish all sex privileges and sex burdens, and would strive to set up the recognition of the common humanity of woman and man as the foundation of law and custom."[17]

REFERENCES

1. Mohanty Chandra, "Cartographies of Struggle: Third World Women and the Politics of Feminism" in Mohanti et al. (ed) *Third World Women and Politics of Feminism*, Blumington, Indians University Press, 1991, 4.
2. Astellara Judith—www.yahoo.com.
3. Roxanne Dunbar—www.yahoo.com.

4. Funk and Wagnet—www.yahoo.com.
5. *Webster Dictionary*—www.yahoo.com.
6. Hélèn Cixous, *Castration or Decapitalism*?, Manchester University Press, 1987.
7. Hélèn Cixous, *Castration or Decapitalism*? Manchester University Press, 1987.
8. Hélèn Cixous, *The Laugh of the Medusa*, Manchester University Press.
9. *Ibid.*
10. Hélèn Cixous, *The Newly Born Women*, Manchester University Press, Manchester, 1987.
11. *Ibid.*
12. Maya Spaces, Patricia, *The Female Imagination*, Centri Press, New York, 4-5.
13. Cheri Register, "American Feminist Literary Criticism: A Bibliographical Introduction," Josephine Donovan (ed.) *Feminist Literary Criticism*, University of Kentucky Press, 1979.
14. Jefferson and Robey, 1986, 209.
15. Ti-Grace Atkinson, *Amazon Odyssey*, Links, New York, 1974, 52.
16. Sushila Singh, *Feminism: Theory, Criticism, Analysis,* Pencraft International, Delhi, 2004, pp. 21-22.
17. *Ibid.*, p. 24.

5 Feminist Literary Criticism

Feminist literary criticism has been defined as a political act whose aim is not simply to interpret the world but to change it by changing the consciousness of those who read and their relation to what they read. The first act of a feminist critic is to become resisting rather than an assenting reader and, by this refusal to assent to begin the process of exorcising the male mind that has been implanted in men and women. This has led to the creation of a new kind of knowledge rendering visible, hitherto invisible component of 'gender' in all discourses produced by academic disciplines.

Feminist criticism involves an act of revision with major tradition to search for an underlying consistent female tradition and to uncover and interpret the symbolism specific to women's writing so that it does not seem as incomprehensible or unimportant as it might when judged by male standards and symbols. It also includes to discover 'lost' works of the past and to reassess male writers from a feminist point of view and finally to become aware of the politics of style and language.

> "By the mid 1970s, feminist criticism was an international movement with a wide, conflicting range of theoretical concerns. Indeed, the potential partners for a feminist critic are a narrative of contemporary critical methods and the quarrels among them. To each partner, the feminist critic brings her questions about women and gender."[1]
>
> —Catherine R. Stimpson

Feminist literary criticism has given us an opportunity to look at 'women' in literature from women's point of view. This reminds us of John Stuart Mill's observation: "We may safely assert that the knowledge that men can acquire of women, even as they have been and are, without reference to what they might be, is wretchedly imperfect and superficial and will always be so until women themselves have told all they have to tell."[2]

In fact feminist criticism is concerned with 'woman' as the producer of textual meanings with the history, themes, genres and structures of literature by women. It has two basic premises: one, 'woman' presented in literature by male writers from their own viewpoint known as phallocentrism and two, 'woman' presented in the writings of female writers from their point of view, that leads to Gynocriticism. Theoretical foundation of feminist criticism is said to be laid by Simone de Beauvoir's book titled, 'The Second Sex'. Elain Showalter said, 'In its earlier phase, feminist criticism concentrated on exposing the misogymy of literary practice: the stereotyped images of women in literature, abuse or textual harassment of women in classic and popular male literature and the exclusion of women from literary history."[3]

She further explains the difference between woman as consumer and woman as the creator of literature. She said, "The feminist critique is essentially political and polemical, with theoretical affiliations to Marxist sociology and aesthetics; gynocritics is more self-contained and experimental, with connections to the modes of new feminist research."[4] In a dialogue between these two positions, Carolyn Heilbrun, the writer, and Catherine Stimpson, editor of the *American Journal* signs: women in culture and society, compare the feminist critique to the Old Testament, looking for the 'sins and errors of the past' and gynocritics to the New Testament, seeking 'the grace of imagination'. "Both kinds are necessary", they explain, for only the Jeremiahs of the feminist critique can lead us out of the 'Egypt of female servitude' to the promised land of the feminist vision. That the discussion makes use of these Biblical metaphors points to the connections between feminist consciousness and conversion narratives which often appear in women's literature. Carolyn Heilburm comments on her own text, 'When I talk about feminist criticism. I am amazed at how high a more tone I take."[5]

The feminist believe that in order to understand woman's position in the world, one has to understand the system of patriarchy. Men all over the world looked at women from their point of view. And they have also taught and even forced women to look at themselves from male point of view. No wonder that Hélèn Cixous has reiterated the demand for self-assertion by women writers and leaders of the feminist movement in unequivocal terms: woman must put herself into the text as into the world and into history by her own movement. It would be a mistake to assume that everything has changed. The goals of the feminist movement have not been achieved, and those who claim we're living in a post-feminist era are either sadly mistaken or tired of thinking about the same subject. Feminist writers refuse to accept the 'images of women' as portrayed by male writers. They are of the view that women characters portrayed by men in literature are lacking in authenticity as women have not experienced their own experience. The very concept of masculinity and femininity are social constructs. She suggests that social and cultural contexts of a work of art should be taken into account in order to understand it in its proper perspective. Feminist literary critics argue that if one studies stereotypes of women, the sexism of male critics, and the limited roles women play in literary history, one would not learn what women have felt and experienced but what men have thought women ought to be.

Gynocritics seek to formulate a female framework for the analysis of women's literature 'to develop new models based on the study of female experience, rather than to adopt male models and theories. Gynocritics take into account the feminist research done in every field. Working as 'gynocritics' women had tried reading male-created texts and producing a literary category as 'the women-centred criticism'. 'The feminist critique' involves the feminist as a reader offering different interpretations of the images of women projected in the male-created texts. Women writers by way of challenging and recasting the male gaze in literature, rewrite and recreate the male-created text from the feminist perspective.

I am inclined to agree with N. Geetha's observation on this subject to a limited extent that feminist writers and critics have keenly felt the complete negation of the female experience in literature. Even the projection of the image of women has been compressed into a few acceptable roles. Women are usually cast into a few popular stereotypes of a narrow range of characterization.

Within feminism, three intellectual traditions have been distinguished, each taking its origin in the 18th century but continuing to operate as differentiating principles even to this day. The first of these traditions to be examined is that of **Evangelical Christianity**. The United States was in the late 18th and early 19th centuries swept by revivals that gave a fresh meaning and significance to religion in this zeal for conversion. Primarily missionary in intent, the movement was eventually led into a concern with social issues, of when perhaps the most significant was the campaign against slavery. More important for our purpose is the extent to which women were drawn in, at first as subordinates, later as active partners. Under its influence women began to emerge from domesticity and take on a public role, as they became increasingly involved in issues of moral and later social reform. Accompanied by ideas of the moral superiority of women, it finds its most modern expression in the 'pro-woman' sections of radical feminism.

The second tradition is that of the Enlightenment philosophers. Among the principles they bequeathed to feminism, is the appeal to human reason rather than tradition and its most influential feminist propagators have been Mary Wollstonecraft and John Stuart Mill. Within this tradition differences between men and women are seen as shaped by the environment rather than as natural, and its whole tendency has been to emphasize the potential similarities between the sexes, rather than the differences. It is from the Enlightenment thinkers, too, that the feminists draw their emphasis on self-realization, freedom and autonomy.

Socialist feminism has its roots, not in Marxism, but in much earlier tradition of communitarian socialism and derives chiefly from the Saint-Simonian Movement in France. The Saint-Simonians were significant for feminism, because of their attacks on the traditional family and their advocacy of a system of communal living that would take the burden of child-rearing away from the individual and place it on the community. Alongside these changes in family life, went changes in the sexual relations between men and women, often described as free love.

It is not suggested that there are three different feminist movements, although feminist groupings are often characterized by an adherence to one or the other of these three traditions. Deriving from separate origins, representing different goals and holding very desperate images of women and their proper place in society, those three traditions comprise the several faces of feminism with which this study is concerned.

It must be admitted that in spite of the early example of Mary Wollstonecraft and her influence, feminism as a social movement was slower to start in India than in the United States. The battle for legal rights was an important aspect of the early feminist movement in both the countries. Without a legal identity of her own, a deserted or ill-treated wife was unable to use the law to defend her interests. Moreover, within marriage she had no rights over her own person, her own property, her earnings and even her own children. It was not difficult, either in India or the United States, to collect examples of husbands who squandered their wives' property, abused them physically or denied them access to their young children. What is more, there was no protection for the wife in the knowledge of her own innocence, since these rights belonged to the husband. Indeed, it was perhaps this more than anything else that aroused the anger of the feminists, but the sympathy of women uncommitted to the feminist cause and of the men who helped to change the law.

This is made very clear in the feminist writings of John Stuart Mill, who perceived the authority of the husband over the wife as one of domestic tyranny comparable with that of the power of an absolute ruler over his subjects or a slave-owner over his slaves. The struggle to change the legal position of married women was, however, only one of the issues that occupied the early years of the feminist movement. The problem of 'surplus' women, who could never marry simply because there were not enough men to go round was also taken care of.

It remains now to look at the reaction of the feminist movement to the socialist tradition of feminism. They could agree on the need to grant women equal rights before the law and the right to economic independence. Both groups also deplored the sexual oppression of women, and wanted to put an end to the double standard of sexual morality. The feminist, on the other hand, were alarmed by the radical transformation of society envisaged by the socialists, including their unorthodox views on marriage and the family.

Of the three intellectual traditions described here, the socialist tradition was the most whole-heartedly feminist, though it had the smallest part to play in 19th century feminism. The doctrine of equal rights had more obvious links with feminism, simply because it was only a short intellectual step from the rights of man to the rights of woman, but it was a step that many in that tradition in fact refused to make.

REFERENCES

1. Catherine R. Stimpson, "Feminist Criticism", *Redrawing the Boundaries: The Transformation of English and American Literary Studies* (eds.), Stephen Greenblatl and Giles Gum (New York: The Modern Language Association of America, 1992), 191.
2. John Stuart Mill, *The Subjugation of Women*, The M.I.T. Press, 1989.
3. Elaine Ehowalter (ed.), "The New Feminist Criticism: Essay on Women," *Literature and Theory,* New York: Pantheon Books, 1985, 5.
4. *Ibid.*
5. Elaine Showalter, "Towards a Feminist Poetics," *Modern Literary Theory: A Reader* (2nd edn.) (eds.), Philip Rice and Patricia Waugh, London: Edward Amold, 1992, 93.

6 Various Feminist Theories

> "Feminism constitutes the political expression of the concerns and interests of women from different regions, classes, nationalities and ethnic backgrounds ... There is and must be a diversity of feminisms responsive to the different needs and concerns of different women and defined by them for themselves."[1]
>
> —Participant at the Nairobi Conference (1985)

Inscribed within Feminist Theory—as it stands today—are various schools of feminist criticism with their dominant positions and practices. These different schools—Black Feminist school, Lesbian Feminist, Marxist Feminist, Psychoanalytic Feminist and Radical Feminist, Indian Feminist, ECO feminist to name some—signal not the discursiveness of feminist theory but its resistance to closure with its concomitant evils of exclusion and marginalization. Feminist theory does not privilege any one school of feminist thought over the other. In this, it demonstrates both its dislike of patriarchal hierarchization and its openness in acknowledging the various trajectories feminists take in order to combat patriarchy. It seems imperative to many feminists to find ways of explaining why women have not simply united to overthrow patriarchy, and why the so-called feminists find themselves inadvertently colluding with the patriarchal values and the assumptions prevalent in our society. Feminist criticism has allowed that fiction too plays a part in the process of constructing subjectivity.

Different approaches to feminism will offer different analysis of the causes and nature of this oppression and thus of the possible solutions. As it is crystal clear that to understand the psyche of a female it is necessary to understand the Feminism and its related theories that affect and explain it to the certain extent. We know that feminist (either male or female) is a person who believes in the theory of feminism. The fundamental goal of feminist perspective, according to Maggic Humm, is "to understand women's oppression in terms of race, gender, class and sexual preference and how to change it." As such the feminist principle is an 'uncompromising pledge' and an antidote to all types of exploitation and oppression of women kind. There are so many types and ways of expressing feminism, it should feel easy and natural for women and men to embrace rather than run from it.

Liberal Feminist Theory

Liberal Feminist theory is a traditional theory which has evolved from liberalism and seeks to copy the liberal principles of justice, liberty and equality to women, without questioning male power. Mary Wollstonecraft's book, *A Vindication of the Rights of Women*, John Stuart Mill's *The Subjection of Women*, Harriet Taylor's, *Enfranchisement of Women* and Betty Friedan's *The Feminine Mystique* and *The Second Stage* belong to this school. These feminists are visionary architects of liberal feminism who combine feminist ideals with humanist tenets, i.e. gender justice based on humanism. It sees sexism as dysfunctional because it deprives society of one-half of its creative workforce.

The presumption that women belong to the family under the aegis of their husband was central to male liberal theorists. Several scholars have pointed out that Locke's theory necessitates conjugal subordination of women because it is rooted in the concept of private property. The 'individuals' who form a social contract for the protection of their lives, their fortunes and their property are in Locke's and subsequent liberal theorists' view male heads of households. Feminist theorists in the natural rights tradition sought to argue, however, that women were citizens, were 'persons' entitled to the same basic rights as men. Because women were so rooted in the home, however, and subject to male authority therein, it was difficult for even liberal theorists to avoid a critique of the home that had more radical implications than a limited liberal position—that of simply granting women rights—might entail. According to Josephine Donovan, the Enlightenment liberal feminists shared the following basic tenets:

"(1) A faith in rationality with some thinkers, such as Wollstonecraft. Reason and God are nearly synonymous—with feminists such as Frances Wright and Sarah Grimke, the individual conscience is regarded as a more reliable source of truth than any established institution or tradition.

(2) A belief that women's and men's souls and rational faculties are the same, in other words, that women and men are ontologically similar.

(3) A belief in education—especially training in critical thinking—as the most effective means to effect social change and transform society.

(4) A view of the individual as an isolated being, who seeks the truth apart from others, who operates as a rational, independent agent, and whose dignity depends on such independence.

(5) Finally, Enlightenment theorists subscribed to the natural rights doctrine, and while the most important theorists did not limit themselves to demanding political rights, the mainstream of the 19th century women's movement settled upon these demands, in particular the demand for the vote."[2]

Mary Wollstonecraft's Vindication remains a classic of feminist theory. Imbued with revolutionary passion, its rhetoric still rings today in stirring and convincing tones. Its central argument is that women remain enslaved because of a corrupt process of socialization which stunts their intellect and teaches them that their proper purpose in life is to serve men.

Wollstonecraft believes that proper education, proper training in critical thinking, is the most important single item on the feminist agenda. She projects a twofold benefit. First, it will enable women to think clearly and sensibly about their own situation, which will make them less gullible and less likely to forget their own self-interest and to become slavish prostitutes. Secondly, the cultivation of women's powers of critical thinking will enable them to grow spiritually, to develop their souls. Since men and women have the same moral and intellectual core (there is no 'sex in souls') they should receive the same mental and spiritual training. "Wollstonecraft rejects Rousseau's idea that men and women think differently. In this she establishes a central liberal feminist position: reason is the same in all persons. When women do reason differently or incorrectly; it is due to a lack of training."[3]

Sarah Grimke's *Letter on Equality* (1838) presents the most cogent and elegant arguments against women's subordination developed in the liberal tradition. Like Wollstonecraft and Wright, Grimke believed strongly in the efficacy of critical thinking. She asserted that women's natural rights had been denied to them by men, and argued that women and men were moral and intellectual equals. Grimke sees that in order to combat the weight of centuries of received opinion and customs, women are going to articulate and legitimate their own truths. Grimke castigates feminine concern with external appearance and considers that the frivolity of most women's dress means that they will not be taken seriously as dignified moral beings. This theory advocates that women as isolated agents are persons first and only incidentally wives, mother, sisters, and daughters. Since women, indeed all people, are fundamentally alone, they need equal opportunities and government protection to enable them to chart their own course. Mill's 'subjection of women' reflects its author's utilitarian principles and remains firmly in the English liberal tradition. The oppression of half the human race dries up the principal fountain of human happiness, and leaves the species less rich. Women's liberation is justified because it will enable each individual to experience the highest happiness.

There are some basic problems with liberal feminist theory. The first is that a strictly liberal analysis left the private sphere untouched. Most liberal feminists veered towards a radical feminist position, attributing the subjection of women as a class to men and to patriarchal or male-serving systems of education and social organization. This necessarily led them to criticize the domestic sphere, the home, and marriage, but basically they thought that such legal changes as the married women's property acts would equalize women's status within marriage. Another question liberals leave unanswered is whether there really are significant 'ontological' differences between women and men. Mill addresses the question but generally concludes, as do other liberals, that what differences exist are minor and the result of conditioning. As Zillah Eisenstein puts it, they did not seem to consider that women, because of the duties ascribed to them as a class, would necessarily start the race at a disadvantage."[4] Nor did they develop ideas for any institutional alternatives to traditional marriage and motherhood. It remained for Charlotte Perkins Gilman to develop this more radical feminist theory at the turn of the century.

Radical Feminist Theory

Radical Feminist theory is chiefly concerned with the issues arising out of 'pornography, prostitution, sexual harassment, rape and woman battering.' In order to be liberated from sexual oppression, radical feminists prescribe a strategy to 'create an exclusively female sexuality through celibacy, auto-eroticism, or lesbianism.' They are against heterosexuality and traditional roles of women as faithful housewives and child-bearing machines. Shulamith Firestone, a radical feminist who has written *The Dialectic of Sex*, argues that women can be liberated by a biological revolution. Kate Millet insists that the roots of women's oppression are deeply buried in gender system of patriarchy. In her book *Sexual Politics*, she says that women will be liberated only when gender discrimination is eliminated as it is constructed and fostered by patriarchy. This ideology is weak as it separates women from the mainstream rather than integrating them into it. Radical feminism sees the oppression of women as fundamental and the most basic form of oppression. All other forms of oppression stem from male dominance. The purpose of this oppression is to obtain psychological ego satisfaction, and strength and self-esteem.

Dana Densmore made major contributions to the development of radical feminist theory. *Independence from the Sexual Revolution* (1971) made the important point that women's liberation and sexual liberation were not synonymous. Densmore urges that women do not consider sexual freedom the be-all and end-all of liberation. 'Spiritual freedom, intellectual freedom, freedom from invasions of privacy and the insults of degrading stereotypes'—these are more important. In fact, the so-called 'sexual liberation' is another ploy to keep women subjugated. Sex (and, as other radical feminists urged, love) is sold as a magical experience that is supposed to justify otherwise dreary lives. Instead, it functions as an opiate keeping women from thinking about their overall condition. The feminists also held that since marriage is a primary formalization of the persecution of women, they consider the rejection of this institution of marriage, both in theory and in practice a primary work of the radical feminist. The feminists also attacked love as an institution that promotes vulnerability, dependence, possessiveness, susceptibility to pain, and prevents the full development of woman's human potential. Radical feminism, according to Daly, is a process or voyage of 'women becoming'. It is both discovery and creation of a world other than patriarchy. Another important aspect of the feminism articulated by radical women of colour is their concern to retain their radical and ethical roots. In many cases this concern is manifested as a desire to preserve authentic women's traditions, to preserve the history and culture of their mothers. A series of statements by Black, Latin and native American feminists strongly expresses a concern that the mother's culture remain alive and that its moral vision be at the foundation of any feminist change. Retaining connections with the mother's culture means reclaiming 'Our female-identified cultural tradition'. Sushila Singh says, "Radical feminism is a recent attempt to create a new conceptual model for understanding many different forms of social oppression in terms of the basic concept of sexual oppression,... Instead, in what appears to be a regression to conservatism, the radical feminists hold that the roots of women's oppression are biological. The origin of women's subjection lies in the fact that as a result of the weakness caused by childbearing women become dependent on men for physical survival. The origin of the family, thus, is a biological factor ... Consequently, the power relationships that develop within the biological family provide a model for understanding all other types of oppression such as racism and class society. Thus, the battle against capitalism and against racism is subsidiary to the more fundamental struggle against sexism."[5]

Hence, the radical feminists conclude that women's liberation requires a biological revolution. They believe that only through technology women can be liberated from the fundamental inequalities of the bearing and rearing of children. They are in the favour of artificial reproduction. The family's consequent disappearance will abolish the prototype of the social 'role system'. Sushila Singh further says. "The radical feminist conception of human nature is neo-Freudian. ...This is the only feminist theory which argues explicitly that women's liberation also necessitates children's liberation."[6]

Marxist (Socialist) School of Feminism

This type of feminism improves intellectual understanding of relations between class and sex. Friedrich Engel's *The Origin of the Family, Private Property, and the State* and Eli Zaretsky's *Socialist Revolution* point out that women are often looked at and treated as property of man. As such, a woman's position is reduced to that of a commodity meant to be used and disposed. It advocates the economic independence of women. But at the same time there is a serious limitation of Marxist Feminism, that is, it regards the class system of capitalism as the only one cause of women's oppression. Critics like Lillian Robinson and Michels Barrett find a relation between literary and social experience. Their concern is the conjunction of the subject and history as part of discourse. Socialist feminist theory is the result of Marxist feminist's discontent with the gender-blind character of traditional Marxist thought. This theory explains the nature and modes of women's oppression. According to it, women's oppression is deeply embedded in existing social and economic structures. It challenges the power relations in patriarchal capitalist system and argues that equality of opportunity can never be possible in society as long as there are fundamental differences in wealth, privilege and power. Thus, socialist feminist struggle is not against male domination alone but against systems of exploitation which disempower women, it means both against patriarchy and capitalism. Apart from engaging itself with the dominant discourse of sex and gender, the feminist discourse and these theories are conspicuous for generating language of its own. Patriarchy first threatened or prohibited the entry of American women into literature. Feminist critics through these various critical theories have set up to correct such literary misnomers and injustices in many ways. As early as the 1970s, they began to question many male writers' portrayal of women as either whores or madonnas, monsters or saints. It is argued that if a woman writer wants to represent adequate female voices, she should come out of the narrow confines of man-made language which is a trap spread by both men as well as women like Brontë and George Eliot who confirm to male point of view. Socialist feminism links oppression to the class structure, sexism is a way of rewarding the working class male; it gives them control over women. Women's work is less valued because it does not produce exchangeable goods.

Marxist feminism is more appropriately called, 'socialist feminism' to point up that it no longer presents an undiluted Marxism but a Marxism modified by radical feminism. It is based on 'natural division of labour in the family'. The final aspect of Marx's philosophy relevant to feminist theory is his theories of economic value. Engels' *Origin of the Family* (1884) remains the only sustained piece of feminist theory produced in the 'first wave' of Marxism. Engels' determination is that a central solution to this economic imbalance is to give women access to the area of public production, a position understandable in the context of the Marxist theory of material determinism, and one which Sacks and Gough appear to accept. A central concern of contemporary socialist feminism has therefore been to determine the role of the household in capitalist society. The most extensive analysis has revolved around the question of domestic labour and its contribution to capitalism. It was thought that women's work is not worth money, is therefore valueless and is therefore cannot be called work. This fact is the material basis for the inferior status of women in a society in which money determines value. Women, who do this valueless work, can hardly be expected to be worth as much as men who work for money. Housewives, therefore, can have access to a vision of a life of unalienated productive activity. Indeed, such awareness is a source of 'consciousness and strength that drives women into the forefront of revolutionary activity'. Then, the transformation of the household took place and as a result housewives and mothers were given new responsibility for maintaining the emotional and psychological realm of personal relations. Moreover, for women within the 'family work' and 'life' were not separated but were collapsed into one another. The housewife is also cut off from the realm of ultimate political control, and this constitutes another element in her alienation. Finally, her economic dependency on men must be seen as an alienating factor. Nevertheless, the fact that her life and work are much more closely integrated than the industrial workers, the fact that unlike the factory worker she has creative control over her time and space, that she occasionally does truly creative, artistic labour such as knitting and needlework and that as a significant part of her labour. She does interact emotionally with others, provide the basis for a 'relatively unalienated' experience. Mariarosa Dalla Costa, in the 1972 article, goes further by asserting that domestic work not only produces use values but is an essential function in the production of surplus value. The family is the very pillar of the capitalist organization of work.

The feminist standpoint must be rooted in an understanding of 'women's perspective' which itself requires the articulation of an epistemology that grows from women's life activity. In Marxist terms, she sees the material basis of women's existence as constituent of women's consciousness. While women also work for wages, their primarily institutionalized activities are housework and child rearing. Like certain earlier socialist feminists and other contemporary cultural feminists Hartsock concludes that these practices create a consciousness that is relational, contextual, integrative, and life affirming, as opposed to the 'abstract masculinity' engendered by men's activities in the capitalist world of commodity exchange. This consciousness forms the basis of a 'feminist standpoint'. Hartsock's 'feminist standpoint' is derived from women's experience of continuity and relation with others, with the natural world of mind with body, an experience that provides a social synthesis. Women's personal problems have social and political causes—this is the meaning of the feminist slogan 'the personal is political'.

However, socialist feminists believe that liberation of women will come from an equal role in production. But it ignores the fact that the sexual division of labour in the home not only discriminates against women on the job and in political life, but it also perpetuates one-sided development of human personality. Women, as primary child rearers and responsible for the emotional and spiritual development of the family, tend to develop empathy, caring and nurturing skills, but have little opportunity to develop analytic, achievement-oriented skills. The reverse is true for men. And since this sexual division of labour also creates male dominance in the political and economic spheres, the values of caring, nurturance and co-operation are absent from public life. Restoring a balance, within individuals and within social spheres, requires an end to the sexual division of labour in the family. Finally, socialist feminist rejects 'stageism', the mechanical notion that history must occur in some predetermined sequence.

Psychoanalytic Feminist Theory

This theory propagates that the root cause of women's oppression is embedded in Oedipus complex. This perspective is both pro-woman as well as anti-woman and thus leads to perpetuation of sexual politics. This perspective originates from Sigmund Freud's *Three Contributions to the Theory of Sexuality*, *Infantile Sexuality* and *The Transformation of Puberty*. Thus, semiotic or psychoanalytic perspectives have yet to be integrated with social, economic and political analysis. Psychoanalytic theory, which is by and large morally neutral about the desires expressed by the psyche, is criticized as a confirmation and justification of them. In fact there is a strong relationship between feminist criticism and psychoanalysis. Both address the themes of psychic relationship of parents and children; the relation between sexuality and its expression, the instability of identity shared by authors and readers. Their methods are also similar as both feminist criticism and psychoanalysis examine dreams, displacement and transference to explain motivations and 'hidden truths'. Juliet Mitchell, Sandra Gilbert and Susan Gubar etc., are some such women critics who fall in this category.

Olive Banks says, "Moreover not only do many radical feminists still see themselves in some respects at least as Marxists but many Marxist feminists are attempting to redefine Marxism by taking into account in a much more sympathetic way than before of the radical feminist critique of sexism in society. Consequently, the division between radical feminists and Marxist feminists should not be taken too literally. They are ideal-types rather than clear-cut divisions within feminism."[7]

Existentialist Feminist Thought

Unlike Marxist, Radical and Psychoanalytic perspectives, Existentialist thought explains comprehensively women's oppression embedded in 'otherness'. Simone de Beauvoir's *The Second Sex* is the key theoretical text of twentieth century feminism. It offers an existentialist explanation of women's situation. It reveals that woman is defined and established as the 'other' because she is not man. This school of thought raises its voice against the sexual oppression of the patriarchal society. Simone said: "The situation of woman is that she—a free and autonomous being like all human creatures—nevertheless finds herself living in a world where men compel her to assume the status of the other."[8]

Simone de Beauvoir's contribution to feminist theory was her use of the existentialist vision to explain the cultural and political status of women. For De Beauvoir realized that a dialectic obtains within a culture as well as within the individual. In a patriarchal culture the male or masculine is set up as the positive or the norm, where the female or the feminine is set up

as the negative, the unessential, the abnormal, or in short, the others. De Beauvoir speculates that woman's identity as other and her fundamental alienation derive in part from her body—especially her reproductive capacity—and in part from the prehistoric division of labour dictated by the childbearing and rearing function. She sees the female body as inherently alienating because it demands so much of women's energy that it saps their potential for engaging in creative pour-soi activity.

De Beauvoir however, as a true existentialist, sees woman as having a moral choice, one that is nonetheless fraught with anxiety, for it involves an apparent rejection of her femininity. Woman's independent successes are in contradiction with her femininity, since the 'true woman' is required to make herself object, to be the other (246). One feminist in the existentialist tradition who has recently taken a position diametrically opposed to De Beauvoir's is Kathryn Allen Rabuzzi. In *The Sacred and the Feminine: Toward a Theology of Housework* (1982) she argues that we should not denigrate the realm of housework, as de Beauvoir does, but rather see it as the site of a continuing feminine culture. Indeed, in the vein of existentialist theology, which locates transcending reality within the everyday world, she urges that the home can be the site of religious events, where occurs 'hierophany', the revelation of the sacred.

Mary Daly's *Beyond God the Father* (1973) along with her more recent *Gynl Ecology* (1978) are among the most important contributions to feminist theory developed in the second wave of feminism. *Beyond God the Father* is a work written very much within the tradition of existentialist theology. The process of women's liberation is perceived by her as redemptive—both for women and society. The iconoclasm must begin from within. Women must exorcise and reject any sense of otherness that they have internalized. Daly feels that process will be redemptive for society as a whole, because it will provide new avenues through which 'Becoming may come to exist.'

Another important vein of contemporary feminist existentialism comes from the 'liberation' school of theology that has developed in the past decade. Liberation theology is social, political and revolutionary. It perceives evil in social and political terms, and conversely sees redemption, or the liberation of good, as occurring through the denial, refusal, and destruction of institutional and ideological evils. At the center of the theory remains the concept of consciousness raising.

Cultural Feminism

Cultural Feminism is a theory which prescribes that there are fundamental personality differences between men and women, and that women's differences are special and should be. This theory of feminism supports the notion that there are differences between men and women. And it wants to overcome sexism by celebrating women's special qualities, women's way, and women's experiences. It believes that woman's way is the better way. Underlying this cultural feminist theory was a matriarchal vision—the idea of a society of strong women guided by essentially female concerns and values. These included, most importantly, pacifism, co-operation, non-violent settlement of differences, and a harmonious regulation of public life. The result of integrating the feminine into the public world may be a desired feminization of culture. Perhaps the most radical of the cultural feminist positions developed by Stanton was her critique of religion, in particular, Christianity. By the 1890s Stanton had come to the conclusion that it was a mindless reliance on the Bible and its supposed doctrine of women's inferiority, that was the central force in perpetuating an ideology of women's subjugation. Stanton goes further in her search for a cultural tradition that reverses rather than denigrates women. She saw the matriarchate as 'a golden age of peace and plenty' and the patriarchate as the 'source of tyranny, wars and (all) social ills'.

Cultural feminists today believe that the traditional realm of women provides the basis for the articulation of a humane world view, one which can operate to change the destructive masculine ideologies that govern the public world. Contemporary cultural feminists therefore hold that women's political value system may be derived from traditional women's culture and applied to the public realm. A cultural feminist opposes some service on the grounds that feminism is a transformative philosophy rooted in the fundamentally pacifist character of the female-value system.

Many cultural feminists include vegetarianism as an important aspect of women's culture. Cultural separatists see a woman's culture as pacifist and ecologically holistic, unlike men's culture, which is seen as rooted in the prehistoric experience of hunting and meat eating. Many contemporary feminists believe that a feminist political ethic may be derived from women's traditional culture, practice and experience. The social reform tendency in cultural feminist theory is not new. In order to counter the masculine ideology, the feminists believe that women must turn their 'left-handed' world into a subject, into a cultural ideological source. To be 'feminine' or to be a 'real woman' in our society means to be 'the (sexual) property of same man whose name we bear. Conversely, to reject such an identification, to be a woman who belongs to no man is to be invisible, pathetic, inauthentic, unreal.

In rejecting the Bible, therefore, Stanton is rejecting the patriarchate and advocating the creation of new society in which mothers will rule, or at least participate in ruling. Because of their connection with the life-giving force women should be considered 'as sacred as the priesthood', and their perspectives and values welcomed.

Even Gage also calls for the reinstatement of the feminine, indeed the motherly, as deity. According to her, it is through a recognition of the divine element of motherhood that evil will cease—especially towards women. When the femininity of the divine is once again acknowledged, the holiness of the divinity will be manifested. The feminine must be reinstated in our picture of the cosmos. Gage continues, and proclaims that "science now declares the feminine principle to inhere in plants, rocks, gems and even in the minutest atoms" (23).

Gilman suggests a number of radical changes—domestic work should be professionalized, people should be trained in cooking, nutrition and child rearing and should be paid to perform these services. Through such reorganization of domestic labour women will be freed from their current twenty-four hour, wage-less oppression and will work eight hours for pay and they will be free to pursue work as their talents permit. Integration of women into the public world, and integration of the public and private will end male domination of the public and therefore end the androcentric reign, as described by Gilman in earlier works. Moreover, ending the confinement of women in the home will make the public world of the streets safe again for women and children.

Like Woodhull and Goldman, Sanger believed in a woman's right to sexual gratifications and was not afraid to state so explicitly. In this, she was a pioneer, for most feminists of the past from Wollstonecraft to Gilman remained somewhat disinterested in the problems of heterosexual relationships. Goldman was the first American feminist who openly supported homosexual rights. Unlike the 'material' or social reform feminists, Goldman did not believe that women would purify politics. Indeed, she remains something of an anomaly among cultural feminists because her theory does not particularly revere or romanticize relationships between and among women, and because most of her major personal relationships were with men.

The participation of cultural feminists in woman-identified networks helps to explain the matriarchal character of their vision. They believed that women were different and that they had a separate cultural and ethical heritage, described by Fuller and Gilman. Cultural feminists today believe that the traditional realm of women provides the basis for the articulation of a human world view, one which can operate to change the destructive masculine ideologies that govern the public world. Contemporary cultural feminists therefore hold that women's political value system may be derived from traditional women's culture and applied to the public realm. Contemporary feminists are more aware of the need to systematize cultural feminist ideology, and to teach it, than their nineteenth-century predecessors. Cultural feminists today, therefore, bypass the nature versus nurture question by assuming that revolution is a matter of transforming ideology, and that all humans are ultimately educable. Cultural feminism remains one of the most important traditions of feminist theory of somewhat more sophisticated in form and political consciousness today than in the 19th century.

Lesbian Feminism

Lesbian Feminism also evolved in the course of 1970s from an initial period in which the anti-Lesbian attitudes of 'straight' feminists were challenged, to an articulation of theory that reflected Lesbian's own unique life situations. By that late 1970s and early 1980s, Lesbians were arguing that the root of women's oppression was the institution of 'heterosexism'. Like women of colour, Lesbians are victims of double jeopardy, oppressed not only for being women, but also for being homosexual. On the other hand, the positive image of the lesbian as a woman of strength and independence continued as a central thesis of Lesbian feminist theory. As Elsa Gidlow, an elderly Lesbian poet puts:

> "The Lesbian personality manifests itself in independence of spirit, in willingness to take responsibility for oneself, to think for oneself, not to take 'authorities' and their diction on trust. It usually includes erotic attraction to women, although we know there have been many women of Lesbian personality who never had sexual relations with one another. What is strongly a part of the Lesbian personality is loyalty and love of other women."[9]

Another aspect of lesbian feminist theory that became established early in the 1970s was the idea that because woman-to-woman relationships need not involve sex roles, they can become model egalitarian bonds. The 'Radicalesbians', a New York group, prepared the first major statement of lesbian feminist theory. Trying to get away from the concept of lesbianism as a strictly sexual identity, the Radicalesbians argue that the lesbian is really a natural 'unconscious' feminist, a woman who devotes her energies to other women, who refuses to be identified in terms of a man:

> "What is a Lesbian? A Lesbian is the rage of all women condensed to the point of explosion. She is the woman who, often beginning at an extremely early age, acts in accordance with her inner compulsion to be a more complete and freer human being than her society .... cares to allow her."[10]

The lesbian may not be fully conscious of the political implications of what for her began as personal necessity, but her gesture of revolt is really against the limitations and oppression laid on her by the female role. Another article on lesbian feminism also appeared in *Notes from the Third Year.* In 'Loving Another Woman', Anne Koedt interviewed a feminist who had recently discovered her lesbian potential, about her relationship with another woman. In this discussion lesbianism is presented as a very human experience, as a strong desire to sleep with her, to let her know what she was feeling. This article helped dispel the myth of the lesbian as a diseased freak. In various articles Martha Shelley urged further that the lesbian should be seen as a model of the independent woman, "I have never met a lesbian who was not a feminist ....I have never met a lesbian who believed that she was innately less rational or capable than a man." She urges that lesbianism is really "the heart of the women's liberation movement." For, in order to throw off the oppression of the male caste, women must unite— "we must learn to love ourselves and each other", "we must grow strong and independent of men so that we can deal with them from a position of strength."

Eco-Feminism

Eco-Feminism is a theory that rests on the basic principle "that patriarchal ways are harmful to women, children and other living things." Often drawn between society's treatment of the environment, or resources and its treatment of women, in resisting culture, eco-feminists believe they are also resisting, plundering, destroying the Earth. Eco-feminism states that patriarchal society is relatively new, something developed over the last 2000 years or so and that the matriarchal society was the first society. Eisler's book *The Chalice and the Blade* is often considered the 'Bible' of eco-feminism. Other books reflecting the theories of eco-feminism are *God was a Woman*, by Manja Gimbuta and *The Creation of Patriarchy* by Gerda Lemen. Eco-feminism suggests that an end to the oppression of women is bound up with ecological values, and that women should be centrally concerned with ending the exploitation of the ecosystem. Eco-feminism has been particularly strong within radical feminism and within the Green Movement.

One of the main theoretical projects of eco-feminism is to construct new ways of thinking about the relationship between humans and nature, including animals, replacing the dualistic, objectifying mode, characteristic of Western science. Certain aspects of deep ecology theory have been criticized by feminists, such as an uncritical use of sexist language and a view of the wilderness as a masculine preserve where men may realize themselves apart from women. But the most serious critique has been framed by animal rights feminists, who part company with deep ecologists on their willingness to subsume the individual in the whole. There is much to be worked out in eco-feminist theory. Meanwhile, it seems appropriate to end this discussion of current feminist theory by citing a recent eco-feminist manifesto—it serves to characterize the direction in which feminist theory is heading away from the traditional conceptualizations of liberal, atomistic theory toward a more comprehensive view that recognized the interrelationships among all living beings and the right of all to exist.

Postmodern Feminism

Postmodern Feminist perspective is the most complex theory. It is also known as 'French Feminism'. It has its genesis in the work of De Beauvoir's *The Second Sex*. The writings of postmodern critics like Hélèn Cixous, Luce Irigarary and Julia Kristeva transcend the boundaries of feminism and offer to women freedom from oppressive thought. According to Cixous, woman must develop feminine writing to change the male defined world. In other words, woman must write herself by putting into words her 'otherness'. Irigaray agrees with Cixous, that feminine sexuality and the female body are sources of feminine writing but disagrees with her application of male philosophical thought to writing. The strategy prescribed by Irigaray for liberation is that women should join together and speak boldly in the active voice avoiding false security. Kristeva also believes like them that women can overcome binary opposition, phallocentrism and logocentricism by breaking silence, speaking and writing.

Feminism has assumed different configurations in relation to postmodernist approaches. Seen only as an agonistic struggle against all forms of patriarchal and sexist oppression, theoretically it becomes an impossibility. As soon as the oppressional conditions are removed, it ceases to exist. The very concept of equality has undergone tremendous change in the light of the new French feminist theories of difference. Through the process of gynesis, a female discourse has been evolved by deliberate valorization of repressed femininity. The French postmodernist theory of Jacques Lacan, Jacques Derrida and Gilles Deleuze has been used in the process of gynesis. Now all the different strands can be divided into two *relational* and *individualist* theories. Currently relational feminism is being widely accepted as it avoids all the negativism associated with extremities of the individualist theories. The present-day feminist thought encompasses a moral vision and emerges as a holistic, anti-militaristic and life affirming philosophy.

Post-Feminism

Toril Moi has used the term 'post-feminism' to cover the different configuarations of feminism and postmodernism present today. Sushila Singh says that:

> "Present-day feminist theorists believe that strictly speaking feminism is an impossible position. The agonistic definition of feminism sees it as the struggle against all forms of patriarchal and sexist oppression. Such an oppositional definition posits feminism as the necessary resistance to patriarchal power. Logically then the aim of feminism as an emancipatory theory becomes to abolish itself with its opponent in a non-sexist non-patriarchal society, feminism will no longer exist" (Moi, 1988, 5). As such feminism is an impossible undertaking, feminism is committed to the struggle for equality for women, an effort to make women become like men. But the struggle for equal rights historically and politically emphasizes the value of women as they are."[11]

Julia Kristeva suggests a third space for feminism to operate—the space which deconstructs all identity, all binary oppositions. But again in deconstructing patriarchal metaphysics, the risk of deconstructing the very logic that sustains the two forms of feminism—of sameness and difference—cannot be avoided. And therefore the three 'spaces' of feminism are logically and often strategically incompatible. Present-day feminism is a historically specific movement, rooted in French Enlightenment through (Mary Wollstonecraft) and in British Liberalism (John Stuart Mill) and consequently wedded in deeply critical style to notions of truth, justice, freedom, and equality. Toril Moi offers a critique of post-feminism on the ground that it avoids taking sides (1988, 19). Post-feminism represents a particular development of one of the three conflicting discourses of feminism. In its eagerness to please the high priests of post-structuralism and postmodernism, post-feminism takes little account of other forms of feminism, and thus enacts a scenario of exclusion and delimitation. Toril Moi believes that only by attempting the impossible wages of constructing a materialist feminist theory that includes the three feminisms that the feminist criticism can be pushed forward post, the political impasse of post-feminism.

Karen Offen (1988) has grouped the different strands of feminism into two arguments: '*Relational*' and '*Individualist*'. The relational feminist thought proposed a gender based but egalitarian vision of social organization. It mainly featured the primacy of companionate, non-hierarchical male-female couple as the basic unit of society. On the other hand, individualist arguments emphasized the individual, irrespective of sex or gender, as the basic unit. Relational feminism stressed women's rights as women in terms of their childbearing and for nurturing capacities in relation to men. It insisted on women's distinctive contribution to these roles in the broader society. Sushila Singh admits that by contrast, individualist feminist thought emphasized more abstract concepts of individual human rights and celebrated the quest for personal independence, dismissing all socially defined roles.

According to Barrett (2000), post-feminism puts the feminine back into women's sense of identity and 'aspirations' and sometimes incorporates ideas drawn from post-structuralist theory which cut away a good deal of the 'conceptual ground' on which earlier forms of feminism were based, including fixed notions of gender difference, ideas of gender equality, middle-class to either or both that (a) we have moved beyond or (b) come from earlier feminism. An alternative post-feminist discourse emerged in the late 1990s. This view aims to extend rather than reject earlier theorizing and is associated with women of substance. Like post-structuralism, postmodernism and postcolonialism, post-feminism has also been characterized as a break with a previous range of oppressive relations. However, Brooks (1997) argues that just as the 'post' of post-colonialism should not imply colonial relations have been overturned, so post-feminism or postmodernism should not be perceived as suggesting that patriarchal or modernist discourses have been superseded. In this view then, post-feminism is feminism that has been dispersed into other areas of debate too (eco-feminism, cyber-feminism, postmodernism). In this way post-feminism challenges the hegemonic assumptions of earlier feminist epistemologies while remaining an important site of political mobilization.

Black Feminism

Like White feminists, many Black women came to feminism through an awareness that they were being treated as second-class citizens within the civil rights movement. As the Combahee River Collective, a Black feminist group, explained in 1977: "It was our experience and disillusionment within these liberation movements, as well as experience on the periphery of the white male left, that led to the need to develop a politics that was anti-racist, unlike those of white women, and antisexist unlike those of Black and White men."[12]

Bell Hooks amplifies that black women felt they were asked to choose between a Black movement that primarily served the interests of black male patriarchs and a women's movement which primarily served the interests of racist White women. Women of colour have a different cultural history and continue to have a different cultural experience than White women, especially middle-class White women who dominate feminist organisations. Blacks and other women of colour are concerned that these differences should not be ignored or rendered invisible, for this would deny the reality and validity of their identity. White women's ignorance of other women's experience is one of the primary forms of racism that women of colour decry in the women's movement. Many Black feminists point to specific differences in the history of Black and White women's experiences. One is that Black women have rarely experienced the leisure-class White women's problem of being denied access to productive work. On the contrary, 'most black women have (had) to work to help house, feed, and clothe their families'. Black women make up a substantial percentage of the Black working force and this is true for the poorest Black family as well as so-called middle-class family. Beale further points out the unique horrors Black women have had to endure.

Black feminists reject the stereotype of the super-strong matriarchal Black woman as one of the grossest distortions of Black women's experience. As Anpela Davis notes, "The designation of the black woman as a matriarch is a Cruel Misnomer. It is a Misnomer because it implies stable kinship structures within which the mother exercises decisive authority. It is cruel because it ignores the profound traumas the black woman must have experienced when she had to surrender her child-bearing to alien and predating economic interests." Despite the differences between Black and White feminists, many Black feminists are urging that the two groups attempt to negotiate these differences and find common cause. Black poet Audra Lorde bares before us the psyche of the Black women's, "those of us who stand outside the circle of this society's definition of acceptable women, those of us who have been forged in the crucibles of difference, those of us who are poor, who are lesbians, who are black, who are older, know that survival is not an academic skill. It is learning how to stand alone, unpopular and sometimes reviled, and how to make common cause with those others identified as outside the structures, in order to define and seek a world in which we can all flourish."[13]

Because they are united with Black men on issues of race, most Black feminists reject a separatist feminist position. In their 1977 manifesto the Cambahee River Collective states:

> "Although we are feminists and lesbians, we feel solidarity with progressive Black men and do not advocate the fractionalization that white women who are separatists demand ....We struggle together with Black men against racism while we struggle with Black men about sexism."[14]

Black feminist literary theory proceeds from the assumption that Black woman experience a unique form of oppression in discursive and non-discursive practices alike because they are victims at once of sexism, racism and by extension classicism. Black feminist theorists argue that the meaning of blackness in this country shapes profoundly the experience of gender, just as the conditions of womanhood affect ineluctably the experience of race. Precisely because the conditions of the Black woman's oppression are specific and complex, Black feminist literary theorists seek particularized methodologies that might reveal the ways in which that oppression is represented in literary texts. More generally, they call into question a variety of standards of valuation that mainstream feminist and andocentric Afro-Americanist theory might naturalize.

French Feministic Theory

The French Feminists tend to view the patriarchal symbolic order as fascistic and death-oriented. Women and their realities have been denied and destroyed by this order. Because they exist 'outside the symbolic' on the margins of discourse, they remain in an other, different space. From this zone they remain as subversives, who must 'deconstruct' the symbolic order of the phallus. At the same time they must affirm the values and vision of their own other realm of experience, while the patriarchal order is death-oriented, theirs is life-affirming. The French feminists thus arrive via the concept of the dialectic seen in Jacques Derrida's notion of 'deconstruction'—at a position not dissimilar to that proposed by Charlotte Perkins Gitman, especially in *His Religion and Hers*.

Freud, Lacan, Julia Kristeva and Hélèn Cixous have important place in the list of French feminists.

REFERENCES

1. Nilufer Cagatay, Caren Grown, and Aida Santiago, "Nairobi Women's Conference: Toward a Global Feminism?", quoted in Johnson-odim, *Common Themes*, 1986, 325.
2. Josephine Donovan, *Feminist Theory: The Intellectual Traditions of American Feminism Continuum*, New York, 1996, 8.
3. *Ibid.*, p. 10.
4. Eisenstein, *Radical Future of Liberal Feminism*, New York: Longman, 1981, 95.
5. Sushila Singh, *Feminism: Theory, Criticism Analysis*, Delhi: Pencraft International, 2004, 30.
6. *Ibid.*
7. Olive Banks, *Faces of Feminism*, New Delhi: St. Martin's Press, 1981, 229.
8. Simone de Beauvoir, *The Second Sex*, trans. & ed. H.M. Parshley, London: Penguin, 1974, 295.
9. Elsa Gidlow, "Lesbianism as a Liberating Force," 1977, as cited in Faderman, *Surpassing the Love of Men*, 385.
10. "The Woman Identified Woman," *Notes from the Third Year*, 1971.
11. Sushila Singh, *Feminism: Theory, Criticism, Analysis*, Delhi: Pencraft International, 2004, 34.
12. The Combahee River Collective, *A Black Feminist Statement in Hall, Scott and Smith, But Some of US are Brave*, 14.
13. Audre Lorde, 'The Master's Tolls will Never Dismantle the Master's House in Moraga and Anzaldue', Garden City: Anchor, 1981, 99.
14. *Ibid.*

7 Some Popular Terms Regarding Feminism

Feminism has been categorized according to the content into various other categories. They are as follows:

Amazon Feminism

Amazon feminism is dedicated to the image of the female protagonist in fiction and fact, as it is expressed in art and literature and also in sexual values and practices. This term of feminism focuses on physical equality and is opposed to gender role and discrimination against women based on assumptions that women supposed to be, look, or behave as if they are passive, weak and helpless. Amazon feminism rejects the idea that certain interests are inherently masculine or feminine, upholds and explores a vision of heroic womanhood.

Femme Feminism

Femme Feminism is a term for the type of feminism the National Organisation of women represents. It is based on the notion that in order for men and women to be equal, women should be granted special privileges and should not participate in feminism.

Decolonising Feminist

Spivak has used this term as she considers herself not only as a postcolonial critic but also as a 'Decolonising feminist'. She often takes up the role of a teacher of the multi-culturalism. In all these positions, she re-reads and reinterprets texts whose meanings have been established for generations. For instance, she re-reads the myths of Naxissus and Echo in order to define the role of the postcolonial feminist. The figure of Echo helps her to articulate the relationship between the feminist and the subaltern woman. Spivak says that in the absence of vigilance, the feminist's representation of the subaltern woman might remain her own story. She also raises the question 'Who decolonises? And how?

Ruth Frankenberg and Latha Mani suggest that the ambiguity of the prefix 'post' in postcolonial must be stressed. They say that the concept 'postcolonial' needs to be "carefully used to describe moments, social formations, subjects positions and practices which arise out of an unfolding axis of colonization/ decolonization, interwoven with the unfolding of other axes, in uneven, unequal relations with one another."

Moderate Feminism

This term of feminism tends to be populated and used mostly by younger women, who have not directly experienced discrimination. They tend to question the need for further effort, and do not think that feminism is any longer viable and in fact rather embarrassing.

Feminazi

This term was made popular by the radio/TV host Rush Limbaugh. A feminazi is defined by anti-feminists, as a feminist who is trying to produce as many abortions as possible. Hence the term 'nazi'. Here the primary focus is individual autonomy, rights, liberty, independence and diversity. Individualist Feminism tends to widely encompass men and focuses on barriers that men and women face due to their gender.

Materialist Feminism

Materialist Feminism is a movement in the late 19th century to liberate women by improving their material condition. This movement revolved around taking the 'burden' off women in regard to housework, working and other traditional female domestic jobs. It is critical of the essentialism implicit in radical feminism and the historical approach to patriarchy. Materialist Feminism has its roots in Marxism and prioritizes social class as the factor determining the situation of women within capitalism.

Pop Feminism

Pop Feminism is known as the negative stereotypical man-hating ideology. This would be the type of feminism that degrades men in all manners and glorifies women. In this relation the term gynocriticism occurs. But it is severely flawed by its concentration or gender difference alone, to the extent that it could even be argued to encourage 'distorted' readings of women's writing. Nevertheless, Showalter provides the reader with a set of tools with which to work a feminist readings of novels by women. What her theory of Gynocritics encourages is that the reader be alert to issues of gender difference, whilst carrying out her reading. Perhaps the same discipline can be applied to the other differences within feminist discourse. There is no doubt that Showalter's model addresses many of the problems central to women writers and to feminist critics, and although there are many stories left-unturned, Gynocritics offers a serious challenge to traditional male-dominated school of thought.

Gender Feminism

N.O.W. Feminism or the National Organisation for Women represents this term of feministic theory. This theory states that in order for men and women to be equal, women must be granted some special privileges, and men should not be an issue in feminism. N.O.W. feminism encompasses only women and fights to offer special privileges to women with the intent of making women equal to men. Gender theory explores ideological inscription and the literary effects of the sex/gender system. The interest in gender theory is not confined to feminist criticism, but has also appeared in feminist thought. Three goals of gender theory are outlined by Joan W. Scott to substitute the analysis of social constructs for biological determinism in the discussion of sexual difference; to introduce comparative studies of women and men into the specific disciplinary filed, and to transform disciplinary paradigms by adding gender as an analytic category. Gender theory promises to introduce the subject of masculinity into feminist criticism, and to bring men into the field as students, scholars, theorists and critics.

Sex-Positive Feminism

Sex-positive Feminism, sometimes known as pro-sex feminism, sex-radical feminism, or sexually liberal feminism, is a movement that was formed in the early 1980s. Some became involved in the sex-positive feminist movement in response to efforts by anti-pornography feminists, such as Catharine MacKinnon, Andrea Dworkin and Dorchen Leidholdt, to put pornography at the center of a feminist explanation of women's oppression (McElroy, 1995). This period of intense debate and acrimony between sex-positive and anti-pornography feminists during the early 1980s is often referred to as the "*Feminist Sex Wars*". Other less academic sex-positive feminists became involved not in opposition to other feminists, but in direct response to what they saw as patriarchal control of sexuality. Authors who have advocated sex-positive feminism include Rllen Willis, Susie Bright, Patrick Califia, Camille Paglia, Avedon Carol, Betty Dodson, and Gayle Rubin.

Sex-positive feminism centers on the idea that sexual freedom is an essential component of women's freedom. As such, sex-positive feminists oppose legal or social efforts to control sexual activities between consenting adults, whether these efforts are initiated by the government, other feminists, opponents of feminism, or any other institution. They embrace sexual minority groups, endorsing the value of coalition-building with members of groups targeted by sex-negativity. Sex-positive feminism is connected with the sex-positive movement.

Gayle Rubin (1984) summarizes the conflict over sex within feminism:

> "...There have been two strains of feminist thought on the subject. One tendency has criticized the restrictions on women's sexual behavior and denounced the high costs imposed on women for being sexually active. This tradition of feminist sexual thought has called for a sexual liberation that would work for women as well as for men. The

second tendency has considered sexual liberalization to be inherently a mere extension of male privilege. This tradition resonates with conservative, anti-sexual discourse."

Difference Feminism

As stereotypes failed and women's confidence grew, feminist theorists led the revival of Difference Feminism. Working on the assumption that women and men really were different in significant ways, some proceeded to re-examine women's traditional values, while others plumbed the depths of the experience of motherhood. Several theorists concluded that many of the female stereotype were actually quite positive. For instance, women were supposed to be weak, and because that was considered feminine, some were actually afraid to be strong.

Carol Gilligan's research on women's values triggered a surge of interest in the 'different Voice' of the female ethic. Mary Daly argued that women were superior to men, and advocated female bonding and spiritual change. Inevitably, the difference feminists were accused of reinforcing sex stereotypes. Kaminer saw it as an outburst of female chauvinism. Some difference feminists argued that it was those on the other side of the divide who saw women as victims.

Separatists

Separatists are often wrongly depicted as lesbians. These feminists advocate separation from men, sometimes total, sometimes partial. The core idea is that 'separating from men enables women to see themselves in a different context'. Many feminists whether or not separatists think this as a necessary first step for personal growth. However, the permanent separation is not advocated in any case. It is inaccurate to consider all lesbians as separatists. While it is true that they do not interact with men for sexual fulfillment and sexual gratification, it is incorrect to say that they shun all interactions with all men.

Academic Feminism

Academic Feminism has made an impact on the teaching and research carried out in many academic institutions. Women's studies courses have been concerned with revising and challenging a wide variety of academic disciplines including sociology, history and English literature. Academic feminism has been concerned to criticize the 'sex blind' nature of academic knowledge. Within sociology there has been a growing literature on the position of women in society and the development of a specifically feminist research methodology.

Whilst there is no single ideological position writing all feminists, most would accept that the subordination of women to men is the result of socio-economic factors and not the effect of biological determinism. At present, feminism remains a vital and visible social movement, particularly successful in the area of cultural creativity. Despite media references to the post-feminist era, the continuing social inequality of women and its eradication remains at the core of feminism in all its forms.

Womyn

Womyn is one of a number of *alternate spellings* which some promote as a way to remove the perception of gender bias from the English word women. Other variants include wimmin (plural), wom!n, *womb*an and womon (singular), while femal (from *female*) and humyn (human) apply the principle elsewhere. All are pronounced the same as the conventional terms. The earliest use of the term "womyn" attested in the *Oxford English Dictionary* is in the name of a 1975 "womyn's festival" mentioned in a *lesbian* publication.

Feminists who prefer to use these words feel that the terms "woman/women" relate to the historical and ongoing social subordination of women, since the word "man" is seen as an exclusively male term, implying that women are a subset of men, or a deviation from the norm. Those who argue in favour of the terms "womon/womyn" contend that they have the right to choose how a term referring to them is spelled, rather than be compelled to use words that evolved in what they see as a *patriarchal society*. Others further argue that "womyn" is based on a medieval spelling of the word, and that returning to the old model of waeman and wyfman meaning man and woman, respectively, would be more egalitarian. Feminists in favour of the modification argue that language is a powerful tool that shapes the way people perceive their surroundings, and even how they understand gender and gender roles. They also feel that the current form of the words do not value women. Therefore, some feminists see these changes as part of a movement to correct what they consider inherent biases in language.

8 Some Feminists: Face to Face

Simone de Beauvoir

Even today in the era of post-feminism, the most important feminist of the West is Simone de Beauvoir (1908-86). She was an existentialist philosopher, left wing political activist and writer of both—fiction and non-fiction. Her pioneering work about the oppression of women—*The Second Sex*—came out in 1949, and was a turning point in her career. She pointed out that womanhood as we knew it, is a social construct; that the inequality of the sexes is not nature's design, but a result of various social forces. She argues that "one is not born but rather becomes a woman."

Novelist, essayist and playwright, Simone de Beauvoir was born in Paris in 1908. The daughter of a lawyer of conservative persuasion, she took a degree in philosophy at the Sorbonne in 1929, placing second to Jean-Paul Sartre. She taught in the Lycees at Marceille and Rouen from 1931-1937, and in Paris from 1938-1943. After the war she emerged as one of the leaders of the existentialist movement, working with Sartre on Les Temps Modernes. Her books include, *The Blood of Others* (1945), *She Came to Stray* (1949), *The Second Sex* (1949), *The Mandarins* (1957), which won the Prix Goncourt, and *Memoirs of a Dutiful Daughter* (1958). One of the most influential thinkers of her generation, Simone was awarded the Austrian State Prize for Literature in 1978. She was regarded as the icon of college women's studies courses, she opined that "marriage is an obscene bourgeois institution," and then easy divorce became a primary goal of the feminist liberation movement.

Woman's first and major limitation is that she is physically weaker than man. More importantly, the values reflected in art, religion, and culture are prescribed by man, not by woman. Consequently, man remains at the centre, driving woman to the margin or periphery. Simone de Beauvoir considered the question as to why, in spite of so much injustice, woman does not dispute male sovereignty. She arrives at the conclusion that in order to fight male-domination, it is necessary for women to organize themselves into a unit. Simone raises a very basic question how did the inequality begin, and why should man have won from the start? She refers to the 17th century feminist Populain de la Barre, who says, "Being men, those who have made and compiled the laws have favoured their own sex, and jurists have elevated these laws into principles." The male uses religion to brainwash the woman into accepting her subordinate position as willed by god himself. Simone de Beauvoir concludes that today's so-called 'inferior' woman is the product of centuries' old discrimination. But she is not pessimistic about woman's future. In her own times she began to perceive a positive change towards equality—women started working, which led to their social and economic freedom. However, she did not forget to warn us that economic equality was not total victory, what was needed was a change in woman's total life pattern. Even the working woman has to reconcile her career with her marriage, which is something that man does not have to do. In spite of her outside work, she has to do household work for the family. De Beauvior rightly says that even after the attainment of equality, women's ideal world would remain different from man's. However, Simone believes that the realization of woman's suppressed potential would be in the interest not only of woman alone, but of entire humanity.

To the emerging activists of the European-women's movement, *The Second Sex* was, in the words of Schwarzer, "a beacon which Simone de Beauvoir lit to show women in the second half of (the twentieth) century, the way!" In the United States feminism emerged through student movements for social change. Some of these active young women dedicated a collection of their writings to Simone de Beauvoir, claiming that it was she who gave them their feminism.

The emerging feminists were inspired not only by the ideas in *The Second Sex* but even more by De Beauvoir's personal life. In her personal life De Beauvoir lived with her lover and comrade—Jean Paul Sartre—but she never married him. Even more inspiring was her decision to deliberately remain childless so that she could dedicate herself freely to the cause of women's liberation, for which she had to teach, travel, write or join a political movement. All this made her a role model of the liberated women, who exemplified that if a woman was determined enough, she could live life on her own terms. Over the years, some of De Beauvoir's ideas have been criticized. For instance, feminists like Germaine Greer have seen strength and potency in woman's body and maternity, but De Beauvoir saw these as handicaps.

Simone de Beauvoir also joined the campaign for women's liberation in France. In 1971 she signed a petition for legalized abortion in which as many as 434 French women openly conferred that they had abortions. She finally declared herself to be a feminist in 1972, at the age of sixty-four, after contributing so significantly to the woman's cause.

In an interview conducted by Chandra Holm for *Indian Review of Books* (2000) Shashi Deshpande says that just as Virginia Woolf's *A Room of One's Own* changed the world for Chandra Holm, *The Second Sex* did the same for her. She says:

> "Oh, Yes! That and for me the book 'The Second Sex' by Simone de Beauvoir. That was also like a flash of light. Fortunately, I read these books after I had started writing. The ideas and thoughts were already in my mind. Reading those books were like a sort of confirmation."[1]

Kate Millett

Kate Millett, another major (the ambivalent feminist) American feminist, was born in 1934 (Sep. 14) and it was in 1970 that her most famous work, recognized as her contribution to feminism, *Sexual Politics*, came out. She applies a feminist perspective to sexual relations between men and women and argues that sex is not a purely biological and isolated act. To a large extent, it has a political aspect, which is quite often neglected. In patriarchal states, and all modern states are patriarchal, men dominate women in bed, as much as they do in other walks of life. Millett's perspective is not only literary, but cultural as well. Millett adopted a totally new method in order to prove her point of view. She had gone through the fiction of Henry Millen, Norman Mailor, D.H. Lawrence and Jean Genet and then analyzed the role of power and domination in the sexual act. She concludes that the sexual act appears to be biological in nature, but in reality it is deeply set in the larger context of human affairs. Consequently, all the other attitudes and values to which that specific culture subscribes and which are present in the man-woman relationship outside the sexual context, are to be found in the microcosm of the sexual act. Miller's other books include *Sita* (1977), *The Basement* (1980), *Going to Iran* (1982), *The Loony-Bin Trip* (1990) and *Politics of Cruelty* (1993). Her point of view is that extra-biological factors determine the nature of sexual relation between various couples.

Millett assails romantic love (a means of emotional manipulation which the male is free to exploit), calls for an end to monogamous marriage and the family (Patriarchy's Chief institution) and proposes a sexual revolution that would 'bring the institution of patriarchy to an end'. When *Sexual Politics* was published, Millett was 34, an unknown sculptor and activist living the life of an impoverished bohemian in New York, Bowery district. Born as Katherine Murray Millett in St. Paul Minn, Millett led a far different life than her strict Catholic parents had envisioned. Married to Japanese Sculptor Fumio Yoshimura, to whom she dedicated *Sexual Politics*, she maintained open relationships with a series of women. She was brilliant, articulate, attractive, passionate in her activism, generous with her time and surprisingly gracious in interviews. *Time* magazine hailed her as 'The Mao Tsetung of Women's Liberation'.

Betty Friedan

Betty Friedan is probably the one feminist who is most relevant to the predicament of the middle-class woman in India. Her most important work, *The Feminine Mystique*, which is set in the second wave of American Feminism, came out in 1963. Friedan was more concerned about the educated, middle-class woman of America. These women apparently had everything that was supposed to make them happy and comfortable, but somewhere something haunting was there. Interestingly, the women themselves could not trace the source of this secret dissatisfaction, they felt guilty about it.

Betty Friedan herself was one such wife. However, there was a slight difference. While other women were merely housewives, Friedan wrote occasional articles for popular magazines. As a part of her job, she also had to interview women. During one such assignments in 1957 she circulated an intensive questionnaire among her former Smith College classmates, whom she was meeting after fifteen years. Friedan's questions were about their present-day lives, their problems and satisfactions. While analyzing the answers, she realized that most of them were not only similar, but also identical. This close similarity, even uniformity, among her respondents puzzled her, she decided to trace the root cause. Out of this search and struggle was born Friedan's memorable work, *The Feminine Mystique*.

In 1965 Friedan formed the National Organisation for Women (NOW) in Washington, to fight the injustice under which women suffered. People believed that the most oppressed group in Western societies was 'women' and the greatest benefit men received was from their sexual exploitation. According to her, patriarchy, more than capitalism, was responsible for women's oppression. Monogamy, marriage, child rearing, the nuclear family were all patriarchal traps to contain and oppress women. When the feminist movement burst into the American social scene in the 1970s, the rallying cry was 'liberation'. The feminists demanded liberation from the role of the housewife and mother who lived in what Betty Friedan famously labeled a 'comfortable concentration camp'. Feminist ideology taught that the duties of the housewife and mother were (in Friedan's words) 'endless, monotonous, unrewarding' and 'peculiarly suited to the capacities of feeble-minded girls'. Society's expectation that a mother should care for her own children was cited as oppression of women by our male-dominated patriarchal society from which women must be liberated so that they can achieve fulfillment in workforce careers just like men.

As a journalist Friedan always looked for some fresh and unusual topic to write on. *The Feminine Mystique* thus served an important social need at the American woman's cost. One day Friedan happened to listen to an informal talk among women, and she realized that at the core of all these complaints, there lay a problem of identity—a stunting or evasion of growth that is perpetuated by the feminine mystique. She further realized that in spite of our modern ways of life, material progress and progressive ideas, we still treated women like Victorians who did not permit their women to gratify their basic needs, did not allow them to grow and fulfil themselves as human beings.

Germaine Greer

Greer had been a rebellious, who went on to become an intellectual celebrity who renounced the church, advocated rampant sexual freedom for women, trashed marriage and the family and fulminated against the imposition of Western values on indigenous peasant cultures throughout the world. Gloria Steinem recalls her with warmth, shrugging off the way Greer disparaged feminist activists in her fabulously successful 1970 book, *The Female Eunuch*. Members of the media (*Life* magazine) dubbed her a 'saucy feminist that even men like'. She has recanted the doctrine of free love and now condemns all men as brutal, lazy sperm factories, incapable of offering women emotional or sexual satisfaction. The bold liberationist once scolded women for not stepping up to the plate and claiming the professional opportunities.

Greer was born in 1939 at Melbourne Victoria. After education at the Star of the Sea Convent in Gardenvale, and then winning a Teacher's College Scholarship, Greer enrolled at

Melbourne University in 1956. The publication of her classic 1970 book *The Female Eunuch*, made her a household name associated with women liberation and radical feminism. She claimed that her book was a part of the Second Feminist Wave. However, other feminists of this wave were reluctant to welcome her because Greer celebrated the delights of heterosexual intercourse. This was at a time when many feminists viewed men as enemies and advised separation from them. Greer was not only highly misunderstood, but it was even given out that under the guise of feminism, she only advocated free love. Although Greer claimed that there were very few feminists who had a viable programme for women's liberation, and that she was one such feminist, her feminism, was a bootstrap kind of feminism. She insisted that it is up to the individual woman to transform herself. Greer argued that the natural differences between men and women had been exaggerated due to social factors. She borrowed Simone de Beauvoir's central thesis, agreeing that 'woman' is a social construct devised by man. She added that women try hard to fit themselves into this model and, in the process, lose their natural human qualities.

She rightly pointed out that the stereotypical female is a sexual object, she must look happy and her face must not betray human or intelligence. She must be completely passive in the sexual act. This desexualization involves not only her body but also her mind and feelings. Thus the ideal woman is a castrated creature, a female eunuch.

Although Greer made a very convincing analysis of women's neutrality, she offered no specific formula by which women could regain their lost human qualities and become their natural 'selves'. An apostle of female physicality, energy, daring experimentation, independence and vigour, she only advised women to take possession of their body and regale in its power, and boldly accept its laws of loveliness. She implored woman to avoid such make-up or clothing that made them look artificial, she also advised them not to marry or live in a monogamous relationship. She believed that love need not necessarily be exclusive, it can exist outside marital relationship. In short, for

Greer, her body was the only effective means that a woman possessed; she could use it to attain emancipation.

Then Greer published *Sex and Destiny*, in which she seemed to have become more status quoist. However, she herself did not accept this criticism and in a later interview said that she remained commenced that monogamy is no more natural for the female than for the male. Other books by Greer include *The Obstacle Race, The Fortunes of Women Painters and Their Works* (1979), *The Madwoman's Underclothes, Essays and Occasional Writings* (1986) and *The Change: Woman, Ageing and Menopause* (1991).

Freud and Lacan

According to Freud, we are born biologically female or male but not with a corresponding readymade feminine or masculine gender identity. Attributes of what are considered 'normal' feminine and masculine sexuality are by no means natural or inherent but constructed painfully from the child's interaction with its social world. The central mechanism of this psychic process, according to Freud, is the idea of 'castration'. The first and absolute love for both male and female infants is the mother. This is referred to as the 'pre-oedipal phase' where the child has no sense of corporate or psychic identity.

Under pressure of these castration fantases the boy represses the forbidden desire and identifies with the father as the figure of authority and moral law for girls. The problem is altogether more complicated as Freud points out, that the girls discover that they have been already 'castrated'. This traumatic realization of 'lack' in her and in her mother makes her turn away from the mother towards the father. In doing so she assumes the 'normal' passive feminine sexuality. Freud's strained endeavour to prove the superiority of men has filled the feminists with outrage; yet it is worthwhile to note that his assumptions are a pointer to the psychic mechanism of the patriarchal structure. It becomes difficult to accept the Freudian assumption of women's inferiority based on her lack of the male organ.

Lacan contributes to the feminist thought in his translation of Freud's ideas into theories of language. Lacan renames

Freud's 'Pre-Oedipal Phase' as the 'imaginary', or the 'Mirror Phase'. It is evident from the theories of these two patriarchs that they both insist on genders as a social construct where women are considered to be inferior in their sense of 'lack'. For Freud the lack in women ensures from the biological difference between sexes; Lacan theorises a symbolic order that enacts an equally irresistible subordination of women. He insists that the phallus as symbol or signifier of that order is not to be identified with the real penis; it merely represents the lack of material things and power which produces all language and hence produces us as subjects.

Given these views, feminists have confirmed and questioned Lacan's thinking on two central areas—his negative account of feminine subjectivity and his conception of language as a totalizing and determining order of meaning. In their attempt to rethink patriarchy, feminists working within this framework focus their attention on the intense pre-oedipal attachment of the child to its mother instead of concentrating as Freud and Lacan do, on the relationship with the prohibiting father. Freud was not a feminist. Nevertheless, his perceptions into the organization of human arrangements in the modern world, like those of Marx, offer insights into the nature of women's oppression. Freud wrote about women in several important books and articles. *Three Contributions to the Theory of Sex* (1905) is one of Freud's earliest speculations about women and their process of growth. The first 'contribution' entitled 'The Sexual Aberrations', begins with observations about various psycho-sexual 'inversions', including homosexuality, sadism and masochism.

'Female Sexuality' (1931), the next essay Freud devoted to women, recapitulates and refines, Freud's by then established theory of the girl's maturation process. It is probably the most complete statement of his theory, and the most important from a feminist's point of view. Here Freud begins to stress the importance of the girl's 'pre-oedipal' phase. Freud argues that the bisexual disposition is stronger in the female than in the male. This is partly because the woman has two sexual organs, 'the vagina, the true female organ, and the clitoris, which is analogous to the male organ. The girl's development involves two phases—the early masculine stage and the later feminine one. As she changes in sex, so must the sex of her love-object change.

At this point Freud parenthetically rejects the term 'Electra complex' to describe the girl's eventual attachment to the father. The situation of the two sexes is not simply a matter of role reversal. Freud identifies the girl's early assertive, active phase with a strong maternal bond. That this stage has been analogized to a matriarchal realm is of considerable interest from a feminist point of view. Her arrival at the oedipal phase is therefore accomplished at a great expense. She now assumes the passivity that is considered the essence of true feminity.

The survey of Freud's ideas on feminine psychology lays the groundwork for a review of contemporary feminist Freudian theory. However, it should also be noted that most major feminists of the 20th century—from Charlotte Perkins Gilman, who called Freudianism a revival of 'Phallic Worship', to Germain Greer—have strongly criticized Freud's theories. Other feminists who have joined in this challenge include Viola Klein, Simone de Beauvoir, Betty Friedan, Eva Figes, and Kate Millett. Kate Millett, whose critique in *Sexual Politics* (1970) remains the most substantial negative feminist analysis of Freudianism, also zeroes in on what she sees, as its inherent biological determinism.

Another central feminist objection to Freudian ideas about female psychology is the obvious male bias inherent in them. As Millett notes, "Freud follows the misogynistic western philosophical tradition initiated by Aristotle, which sees women as incomplete males. Like most feminists, Thompson argues that if there is any validity to the idea of penis envy, it must lie in a female envy of the male social status, his power, freedom, and dominance." De Beauvoir similarly argues, if the little girl feels penis envy, it is only as the symbol of privileges enjoyed by boys? De Beauvoir suggests that through them Freudianism became a 'religion', Firestone calls it 'our modern church'. Betty Friedan argues that revisionist Freudianism was the philosophical underpinning that sustained the 'feminine mystique'. Friedan notes:

> "Because Freud's followers could only see woman in the image defined by Freud ....With no possibility of happiness unless she adjusted to being man's passive object—they wanted to help women get rid of their suppressed envy, their neurotic desire to be equal. They wanted to help women find sexual fulfillment as women by affirming their natural inferiority."[2]

Psychoanalysis thus became a central brainwashing device to keep women passive. The rejection of Freudian theory by feminists of the early 1970s was challenged by a new vein of feminist inquiry that developed in the late 1970s.

One could criticize Lacan from a feminist point of view for equating wholeness with the phallus and alienation with castration. While Lacan like Freud reflects a male bias, in particular a similar penis or phallus obsession, the French feminists have seized upon aspects of his theory for their own purposes.

Julia Kirsteva and Hélène Cixous, two of the most important French feminists, have offered unique interpretations of Lacan. According to them feminism has only been but a moment in the process of coming to consciousness about the implacable violence which constitutes any symbolic contract.

Julia Kristeva

French critic, psychoanalyst, semiotician, and writer Kristeva has explored many subjects including structuralist linguistics and semiotics, psychoanalysis and contemporary feminisms. Many of her books have been translated into English. She studied at the University of Sofia and settled (1966) in Paris, where she received (1973) a doctorate in linguistics from the school of Higher Education in Social Sciences. Kristeva, who became a psychoanalyst at 40, is also a professor of linguistics at the University of Paris. In general, she takes a post-structuralist approach, analyzing the relationship among language, society and self with its individual psychology and sexuality. Her books include *Semeiotike* (1969), *Revolution in*

Poetic Language (1974), *Black Sun: Depression and Melancholia* (1987), *Time and Sense: Proust and the Experience of Literature* (1994) and *The Sense and Non-sense of Revolt* (1996). The subjects of her early 21st century trilogy on 'female genius' are Hannah Arendt, Melania Klein and Colette. She has also written two novels.

Although Kristeva does not refer to her own writing as feminist, many feminists turn to her work in order to expand and develop various discussions and debates in feminist theory and criticism.

Kristeva accepts Lacan's theory of the phallocentric symbolic order and concludes that women in the sense of feminine has no access to language. According to her, women's language need not refer to writings by women. Her theory of subjectivity is based on an effect of language which has feminine and masculine aspects. Kristeva's feminist standpoint is in her attempt to locate the negativity and in her refusal pertaining to the marginal in woman.

Kristeva criticises Lacanian theory because it starts more or less with the mirror stage which turns into what Lacan describes as the 'metonymy of desire'. She emphasized the implications of this maternal function which both Freud and Lacan had ignored and which opens up a possibility for treating psychosis which was foreclosed by Lacanian analysis. Kristeva also notes the dilemma women find themselves in vis-à-vis the symbolic, however. Either they can enter it and become functional men or can flee everything considered 'phallic' to find refuge in the valorization of a silent underwater body.

Three elements of Kristeva's thought have been particularly important for feminist theory in Anglo-American contexts:

(1) Her attempt to bring the body back into discourses in the human sciences;

(2) Her focus on the significance of the Maternal and Preoedipal in the constitution of subjectivity; and

(3) Her notion of objection as an explanation for oppression and discrimination.

Theories of the body are particularly important for feminists because historically (in the humanities) the body has been associated with the feminine, the female or women, and denigrated as weak, immoral, unclean or decaying. Throughout her writing over the last three decades, Kristeva theorized the connection between mind and body, culture and nature, psyche and soma, matter and representation.

Kristeva argues that maternal regulation is the law before the law, before Paternal Law. She calls for a new discourse of maternity that acknowledges the importance of the maternal function in the development of subjectivity and in culture. In *Motherhood According to Belline* and elsewhere, she suggests that the maternal function cannot be reduced to mother, feminine or woman. As a woman and as a mother, a woman both loves and desires, and as such she is primarily a social and speaking being. As a woman and a mother, she is always sexed. Kristeva's analysis suggests that to some extent anyone can fulfill the maternal function, men or women. Some feminists have found Kristeva's notion of a subject-in-process a useful alternative to traditional notions of an autonomous unified (masculine) subject.

Juliet Mitchell

Mitchell argued that woman's oppression was linked to four essential social structures: production, reproduction, sexuality and socialization. Mitchell sought to combine a critique of socialist thought and psychoanalysis for feminist theory is what was one of the earliest attempts to make feminism inter-disciplinary, and overtly political. Mitchell, influenced by Lacanian thought, argues that to abandon Freud would be detrimental to the feminist cause, especially since Freud's work was a critique and analysis of patriarchal society. Defending the Freudian theory of castration, Mitchell suggests that fantasy rather than fact determines gender. Definitions of masculinity and femininity are constituted through the symbolic, where man is the self-determining, autonomous agent and the woman is the lacking other. She has written *Woman's Estate* (1971), *Psychoanalysis and Feminism* (1974) and *Feminine Sexuality* (1982).

Elaine Showalter

Calling for new models based on the woman's experience rather than a blind addiction to and adaptation of masculine theories and models, Showalter launched the search for 'gynocriticism'. Gynocriticism should, according to Showalter, look at the history, styles, themes, genres, and structures of writing by women; the psychodynamics of female creativity, the trajectory of the individual or collective female career; and the evolution or laws of a female literary tradition.' In her seminal *A Literature of Their Own* (1977), Showalter analyses the mechanisms through which the women writers were assiduously kept out of the literary canon during the 19th century. The criticism of the time was almost entirely patriarchal in its opinion, rejecting women's texts as limited in range, superfluous and trivial. Showalter detects a double bind on the woman writer of the age—in the first place she was limited to certain themes in her writings by the prevalent male critical opinion. The male literary establishment decided the themes like domestic problems, children, food or fashion for her. Showalter comments, "to their contemporaries, nineteenth century women writers were women first, artists second."[3]

Showalter is a founder of feminist criticism in the United States, developing the concept and practice of gynocriticism. She has written dozens of articles and essays on feminist topics and has edited *Women's Liberation and Literature* (1970), the first textbook on women in literature. Showalter has been a television critic for *People* magazine and a commentator on BBC radio and television. She is the Avalon Founder Professor Emerita. Her academic honours include a Guggenheim Fellowship and a Rockefeller Humanities Fellowship. She is also the former president of the Modern Language Association (MLA). Showalter says that the most constructive approach to future feminist theory and criticism lies in a focus on nurturing a new feminine cultural perspective within a feminist tradition that at the same time exists within the male tradition, but on which it is not dependent and to which it is not answerable.

Showalter coined the term gynocritics to describe literary criticism based in a feminine perspective. The goal of gynocritics is not to erase the differences between male and female writing; gynocritics is not 'on a pilgrimage to the promised land in which gender would lose its power, in which all texts would be sexless and equal, like angels.' Rather gynocritics aims to understand the specificity of women's writing not as a product of sexism but as a fundamental aspect of female reality.

She says that gynocritics may never succeed in understanding the special differences of women's writing, or realize a distinct female literary tradition. But, with grounding in theory and historical research, Showalter sees gynocriticism as a way to 'learn something solid, enduring and real about the relation of women to literary culture.'

Showalter identifies three major phases in the development of women's writing. These three phases are predominantly responses of women authors to the socio-cultural contexts which were patriarchal through and through:

(i) **The Feminine Phase (1840-1880).** Here women writers initiated the male writer's modes. They also assimilated, accepted and finally perpetuated the patriarchal aesthetic through their work. Showalter points out that the women writers of the nineteenth century adopted masculine names or emphasised their marital status. There was an 'all-inclusive female realism' which narrated the exploration of the daily lives and values of women within the family and community.

(ii) **The Feminist Phase (1880-1890).** It extends to around the 1920s. This phase is characterized by Showalter as a protest phase, where women authors rebelled against prevalent patriarchal attitudes. The authors rebelled against the Victorian sexual stereotypes and tried their best to explore the woman's position in terms of work, class and the family. Women demanded autonomy with full force and vigour in this phase.

(iii) **The Female Phase** is the most modern phase for the feminist in the twentieth century. Women writers started their search for their own voice and identity as opposed to the identity 'granted' by patriarchy. Showalter perceives the post-1960s as a heightened female phase. Here there is the double legacy of feminine self-hatred and feminist withdrawal. Showalter detects Freudian and Marxist influences in authors of the female phase.

Eli Zaretsky

Eli Zaretsky is a big name in the Socialist feminist tradition. Zaretsky's work shows a concern with almost all the issues of socialist feminism. Zaretsky argues that capitalism produced a massive split between the public and private spheres. Work and life were separated as material production was separated from private labour performed by women at home. Zaretsky is right to argue that psychoanalysis put forth a new notion of autonomy that was personal, not moral, and that challenged the distinction between public and private. Zaretsky is also right to criticize psychoanalysis for being slow to respond to and even resisting feminism (although he makes only fleeting acknowledgment of the so-called relational psychoanalysts who have made feminism crucial to their thinking).

Eli Zaretsky as a social feminist claims to work for the total transformation of society in the interests of the vast majority of people. Zaretsky joins other socialist feminists whose goals include economic security and justice for all, a dispersion of power so that people control the decisions which directly affect their lives, and an end to exploitation, racism and sexism. They seek to build a society characterized by commitment to working for the common good, and which places high priority on the values of cooperation, nurturance and caring for others. Zaretsky emphasizes that a fully human society cannot be achieved so long as caring, nurturance and emotional development are limited to the female half of the species and so long as personal fulfillment is relegated to the private (or family) sphere of life.

Eli Zaretsky, born in Brooklyn, New York, wrote various articles on the history of the family, psychoanalysis, and modern cultural history. His book *Capitalism, the Family and Personal Life* has been translated into fourteen languages. His latest publication *Secrets of the Soul* is a social and cultural history of psychoanalysis. In it Zaretsky charts the divergent schools in the psychoanalytic community and how they evolved—sometimes under pressure—from sexism to feminism, from homophobia to acceptance of diversity, from social control to personal emancipation. From Freud to Zoloft, Zaretsky tells the story of what may be the most intimate science of all.

Luce Irigaray

Luce Irigaray is and can be categorized as a great resource for human analysis within many spheres, although she is more widely recognized for her feminist texts. She is also trained in Psychology, Psychopathology and Linguistics. Her writings explore a broad spectrum of gender related philosophy. She has managed to capture the essence of sexual difference without causing ignoring amongst the male gender. She philosophizes of a language barrier between men and women, one which has been unrecognized, or ill-informed of between the two sexes until Lucy Irigaray captures them in her discourse. Irigaray's rejection of the male symbolic order in view to highlight difference has been regarded as the 'radical feminist' phase of the feminist movement. Irigaray seeks to uncover a feminine order of meaning so that a sexual identity of the woman may be constructed. Turning to Freud, Irigaray shows how Freud's theory of sexuality is basically premised on one sex—the male. The male is the paradigm of all sexuality—physical changes (Freud, Irigaray points out, speaks of the 'lack' in the females but never speaks of the degeneration of breasts in the males, which should also be construed a 'lack') and sexual pleasure—and sexuality is a priori male for Freud. Irigaray notes: "Female sexuality has always been conceptualised on the basis of masculine parameters." Irigaray suggests a specifically feminine writing practice. Proceeding from the assumption that a different order of meaning is necessary to construct a positive representation of the feminine, Irigaray searches out new linguistic modes of expressing the feminine self. The Lacanian idea that language is phallic, Irigaray argues, implies a dangerous situation. If women are to have their own identity, they must subvert the phallic version of the symbolic. She sees writing as going through the looking glass into a world of woman's self-representation.

She associates the metaphor of the specular mirror with this feminine representation. The curved surface of the speculum produces a deformed image which reverses the reflections of masculine discourse.

Rejecting the primacy of sight in psychoanalysis, Irigaray returns to the pre-oedipal stage where the sense of touch rules the mother-child relation. According to her, Lacanian psychoanalysis which privileges metaphor over metonymy has resulted in the neglect of the feminine sexuality. In her search for the equivalent of the mother-daughter bond, Irigaray has resurrected those aspects of Western culture that symbolize specifically feminine conditions.

Hélène Cixous

Cixous' work has been influenced by Derridean deconstruction. Hélène Cixous was born in Oran, Algeria, to a German Ashkenazi mother and Algerian Sephardic father. She earned her aggregation in English in 1959 and her Docteur on Letters in 1968. Her main focus, at this time, was on English Literature, and the works of James Joyce. She founded the Centre for Women's Studies in University of Paris-VIII, the first in Europe. She has published widely, including twenty-three volumes of poems, six books of essays, five plays, and numerous influential articles. She is considered one of the mothers of Poststructuralist Feminist Theory. This rhetorical movement was fueled by the teachings and writings of three French Feminists: Luce Irigaray, Julia Kristeva and Hélène Cixous.

In the 1970s, Cixous began writing about the relationship between sexuality and language. Like the other poststructuralist feminine theorists, Cixous believes that our sexuality is directly tied to how we communicate in society. In 1975, Cixous published her most influential article, 'La rire de la meduse'. *The Laugh of the Medusa* was translated and released in English in 1976. It is an extremely literary essay and is well known as an exhortation to a feminine mode of writing. It is a strident critique of 'logocentrism' and 'phallogacentrism'. This essay also calls for an acknowledgement of universal bisexuality, or polymorphous perversity, which is clearly a precursor of queer theory's later emphasis, and it swiftly rejects many kinds of essentialism which were still common in Anglo-American feminism at the time. She is most recognized in the United States for developing the concept of 'écriture féminine', as a way of overcoming the limits of Western logocentrism, and for opening new ways to deal with subjective difference in both writing and social theory.

Cixous' life and works is a search for emancipation, for the self and for others. She distinguishes herself from much academic by insisting on celebrating life rather than death. From her early psychoanalytically influenced work concentrating on the individual in search of personal liberation, she has moved toward the collective struggles of women, and an interest in the developing world, and studied the death camps of World War II through the experiences and writing of others. "Censor the body and you censor breath and speech at the same time. Write yourself your body must be heard" (*The Laugh of the Medusa*); "writing as if I had the urge to go on enjoying, to feel, to push, to feel the force of my muscles, and my harmony, to be pregnant and at the same time to give myself the joys of parturition, the joys of both the mother and the child. To give birth to myself and to nurse myself. Life Summons Life. Pleasure seeks renewal" (*Coming to Writing*). These statements show that Cixous uses her poetic genius and academic savy to create a text that is brilliantly effective in many ways. First, she succeeds in giving the reader a concept of feminine writing but convinces us that in actually defining of the term, we destroy its beauty.

REFERENCES

1. Chandra Holm, "A Writer of Substairs", Interview, *Indian Review of Books*, 16 May-15 June, 2000, 5-9.
2. Betty Friedan, *The Feminine Mystique*, New York: Neston, 1963, 119.
3. Pramod K. Nayar, *Literary Theory Today*, New Delhi: Asia Book Club, 2002, 91.

9 Some Major Books on Feminist Theories and Issues

A Vindication of the Rights of Woman, written by Mary Wollstonecraft, remains a classic of feminist theory. Imbued with revolutionary passion, its rhetoric still rings today in stirring and convincing tones. Its central argument is that women remain enslaved because of a corrupt process of socialization which stunts their intellect and teaches them that their proper purpose in life is to serve men. Wollstonecraft has particularly exercised over the empty, frivolous lives that upper class leisured women were encouraged to lead. As they thought that strength of body and mind are sacrificed to libertine notions of beauty, to the desire of establishing themselves—the only way women can rise in the world—by marriage.

Wollstonecraft is aware that women must cultivate their beauty and their senses at the expense of their minds, because their only means of establishing themselves economically and of obtaining a measure of power is by attracting a husband. To rise in the world they must marry advantageously and to this object their time is sacrificed, and their persons often legally prostituted. To quote:

> "Pleasure is the business of woman's life—they have, to maintain their power, resigned the natural rights which the exercise of reason might have procured them, and have chosen rather to be short-lived queens than labour to obtain the sober pleasures that arise from equality."[1]

> "She was created to be the toy of man, his rattle and it must jingle in the ears whenever, dismissing reason, he chooses to be amused."[2]

Wollstonecraft made it clear here that women's sole purpose is therefore to cultivate the non-rational, sensuous side of life in order to please men. Such a role, according to Wollstonecraft, lacks dignity.

The Second Sex is best known work of Simone de Beauvoir and was a seminal text in twentieth century feminism. It is a work on the treatment of women throughout history and often regarded as the major feminist work. In it she argues that women throughout history have been defined as the 'other' sex, an aberration from the 'normal' male sex. It paved the way for the second wave feminism. This lengthy study of the sources of women's inequality, still a cornerstone of feminist theory, made Simone a feminist icon for the rest of her life. De Beauvoir's primary thesis is that "men fundamentally oppress women by characterizing them on every level, as the 'other', defined exclusively in opposition to men. He extends out into the world to impose his will on the world whereas the woman is doomed to immanence or inwardness. He creates, acts, invents; she waits for him to save her."[3] This distinction is the basis of all later arguments of Simone.

This book explains various mythical representation of women and demonstrates how these myths have imprinted human consciousness often to the disservice of women. She hopes to debunk the persistent myth of the 'eternal feminine', by showing that it arose from male discomfort with the fact of his own birth. Throughout history maternity has been both worshipped and reviled—the mother both brings life and heralds death. She insists on the impossibility of comparing the 'character' of men and women without considering the differences in their situation, and in Book II, entitled *Woman's Life Today* she turns to the concrete realities of the situation. She traces female development through its formative stages—childhood, youth and sexual initiation. Her goal is to prove that women are not 'Born' feminine but shaped by thousand external processes. She shows how, at each stage of her upbringing, a girl is conditioned into accepting passivity, dependence, repetition and inwardness. Every force in the society conspires to deprive her of subjectivity and flatter her into an object. Denied the possibility of independent work or creative fulfillment, the women must accept a dissatisfying life of housework, childbearing and sexual slavishness.

Having brought the woman to adulthood, De Beauvoir analyses the various situations, or roles, the adult woman inhabits. The bourgeois woman performs three major functions—wife, mother and entertainer. She also reflects on the trauma of old age when a woman loses her reproductive capacity, she loses her primary purpose and therefore her identity. In the final chapter 'Woman's Situation and Character', she reiterates the controversial claim that woman's situation is not the result of her character rather her character is a result of her situation.

The Madwoman in the Attic is written by Sandra Gilbert and Susan Gubar. In this book, Gilbert and Gubar locate the female territory in its larger context and examine the borders along which the woman writer defined herself. Through this book feminist criticism has established the historical relativity of the gender definitions that organize this culture. This book dwelt on inter-women discourses. According to Gilbert and Gubar, "just as Literary sons suffer an anxiety of authorship and Oedipal struggle with male precursors, woman too write in confrontation with culture and with themselves by creating an author's double: the madwoman in the attic."[4]

No Man's Land (1988), another notable work by the authors, fostered a more pluralist feminist criticism than the singular psycho-analytical model of Mad woman. In this work, "the two authors discussed how Lesbian expatriates in Paris, 'reinvented gender' and explored the consumerism of the Gilded Age in an informed materialistic analysis"[5] and described the sexual imagery of imperialism. This work expressed the feminist conviction that 'male' and 'female' are fictive constructs variously shaped by cultures.

A Criticism of Our Own: Autonomy and Assimiliation in Afro-American and Feminist Literary Theory (1989), written by

Elaine Showalter, chronicles the differences among feminist critical practices and among the theoretical movements they represent. It outlines the dominant feminist methodologies of the 1980s. Showalter shows the six kinds of projects based on her earlier versions:

"(1) androgynist poetics, dedicating to effacing gender differences;
(2) the feminist critique of male culture;
(3) a Female Aesthetic celebrating women's culture;
(4) gynocritics, or the study of the tradition(s) of women's writing;
(5) gynesic, or poststructuralist feminist—criticism, focusing on 'the feminine' as a category within culture; and
(6) gender theory."[6]

At the end of her essay, Showalter declares that there is an urgent necessity to affirm the importance of Black and female thinkers, speakers, readers, and writers. Showalter parallels the evolution of African-American criticism and feminist criticism in the 1980s.

Sexual Politics, published in 1970, by Kate Millett is her first major work, which according to feminist social scientist is "one of the first major attempts to provide a thorough theoretical examination of the oppression of women using the concept of patriarchy." The growth of the feminist movement is inseparable from feminist criticism as the increasing consciousness of women lead them to question and criticize misrepresentation of women. To understand the ways in which gender is acquired through language and to perceive the role played by the language in creating women's subjectivities and their oppressions are the two important tasks which the feminists set for themselves.

Kate Millett urges that it is just as probable that the girl, invested with 'childish narcissism', take her own body as norm. Freud did not see his patients' dissatisfaction as a 'justified' reaction to 'the limiting circumstances imposed on them by society, but as symptomatic of an independent and universal feminine tendency—Penis envy' Gynocritics draw upon Millet's theory of sexual politics or the power struggle in a man-woman relatioinship and made out a case for the woman characters in the novel. Even in literature, the treatment of women focuses upon their sexuality. Kate Millett writes in her *Sexual Politics*,

> "Literature has observed not only the truthful explicitness of pomography, but its anti-social characters as well. Since this tendency to hurt or insult has been given free expression, it has become far easier to assess sexual antagonism in the male."[7]

The Feminine Mystique by Betty Friedan (1963) attacked the popular notion that women during this time could only find fulfillment through childbearing and homemaking. The book has been the subject of controversy. The chapter one 'The Problem that has No Name' speaks about traditional women. It says, "Over and over women heard in voices of tradition and of Freudian Sophistication that they could desire—no greater destiny than to glory in their own femininity." The second Chapter 'The Happy Housewife Heroine' speaks about the feminine mystique that began to spread through the land. The feminine mystique says that the highest value and the only commitment for women is the fulfillment of their own femininity. It says that the great mistake of Western culture, through most of its history, has been the under valuation of this femininity. It says this femininity is so mysterious and intuitive and close to the creation and origin of life that man-made science may never be able to understand it. But however special and different, it is in no way inferior to the nature of man; it may even in certain respects be superior. The mistake, says the mystique, the root of women's troubles in the part is that woman envied men, women tried to be like men, instead of accepting their own nature, which can find fulfillment only in sexual passivity, male domination, and nurturing maternal love. The feminine mystique is so powerful that woman grow up no longer knowing that they have the desires and capacities the mystique forbids. But such a mystique does not fasten itself on a whole nation in a few short years, reversing the trends of a century, without cause.

The core of her thesis is that woman's problem today is not sexual but a problem of identity. "Our culture does not permit women to accept or gratify their basic need to grow and fulfill their potentialities as human beings, a need which is not solely defined by their sexual role."[8]

The Newly Born Woman written by Hélène Cixous, was published in 1987 (Manchester University Press, Manchester). This book applies poststructuralist and psychoanalytical theory in an analysis of the potential for women to subvert theoretical and social structures. For Cixous, 'Woman' is the product of linguistic difference (e.g. binary oppositions such as culture/nature, activity/passivity) but the 'feminine' is a source of energy and diversity. For example, 'feminine writing' (not always by women) which operates on difference and plurality, can display the diversity and transgression of 'Libidinal femininity'. This book further explains that the male is active and looks in comparison to the passive female who is merely observed. "Femininity is therefore only present as it is observed by the male and crucially, while the feminine is the other to the masculine, the male is interested in this other only, in order to return to itself—that is to say that the masculine desire for woman is ultimately a self-love. The woman is therefore excluded from patriarchal culture, and not only this, she is a non-presence even to herself. The woman is separated from her own body and her own desires. The woman simply cannot make sense of herself in a language that is designed to articulate and conceptualise masculinity."[9] Unlike Freud who saw female sexuality as a 'dark continent' that had not yet been explored, Cixous in *The Newly Born Woman* sees female sexuality as something that is likely to be apparent in a woman's written text. Cixous aims for her readers to understand the nature of women's writing as much from the way in which she writes, as from what she writes about.

The Laugh of the Medusa, as its title suggests, is a wonderful essay written by Hélène Cixous. She urges us to embrace 'difference' and to use it. She focuses on the relationship between feminine libido and feminine writing. Her work stresses on feminine sexuality that is plural and so is feminine writing.

The book proclaims, "The future must no longer be determined by the past." "I shall speak about women's writing, about what it will do. Woman must write herself, must write about women and bring women to writing, from which they have been driven away as violently as from their bodies for the same reasons, by the same law, with the same fatal goal. Women must put herself into the text—as into the world and into history—by her own movement."

Speculum of the Other Woman is written by Luce Irigaray and was published in 1974 (Ithaca, N.Y., Cornwell University Press). This book is, however, her first major theoretical work. The 'speculum' of the title is a curved mirror used to examine a woman's sexual organs. The book is a challenge to psychoanalysis and specifically to the way in which the mother-daughter relationship is announced for in Freudian and Lacanian theory. Female sexuality, on the Freudian model, is accounted for as divergence from the masculine norm, most precisely in the theory of penis envy. No positive value is given to the female sex organs and thus any demand for female equality, however well-motivated it may be by concern for the political and economic plight of women, capitulates to this patriarchal symbolic order, for it immediately assumes that women lack something that men already have. The symbolic order presents women merely as potential mothers, and not as autonomous subjects. In being refused access to language and to society, women run a greater risk of psychosis and a fall into a private language in which women can communicate with women.

Gender Trouble: Feminism and the Subversion of Identity is written by Judith Butler in 1990. It is arguably the most influential theoretical text of the 1990s. This book distills forty years of French theory—from pioneer feminist Simone de Beauvoir to Julia Kristeva, and from Jacques Lacan and Louis Althusser to Jacques Derrida and Michel Foucault—to explore how gendered identity is socially produced through repetitions of ordinary daily activities. Butler proposes here that we understand 'sex' and 'gender' as citational repetitions. Various cultural discourses converge in a prevailing understanding of what 'boy' and 'girl', 'man' and 'woman' signify. In Butler's view, we feel our way into these roles, slowly establishing through under the vigilant eyes of mighty social forces, the way we will occupy them. Given our prevailing categories, we experience this process as discovering our identity. Butler believes identity is a trap, a hardening into rigid, binarized categories of much more fluid and heterogeneous possibilities. However, if we apply Butler's observations to the current postcolonial approach toward the female condition, we will invariably find an element of deliberate shying away from the specific cultural conditions that perpetuate discriminating behaviour towards women.

This Sex which is Not One by Luce Irigaray (Ithaca, N.Y., Cornwell University Press) was published in 1977. It explores these issues of feminism further. "Feminine sexuality, sexual pleasure and desire are analysed. Female pleasure lies in touching, rather than in the masculine pleasure of looking. Irigaray asserts here that due to uterus, vulva, breasts and lips of the vagina; the women have 'sex organs more or less everywhere.'"[10] The woman is plural and as such is not confined within a masculine culture that is seen to counter everything in units. Female pleasure is therefore other to the patriarchal culture, and cannot be contained within its economy of looking that makes the woman passive. Irigaray's subsequent writing has explored the possibility of a feminine writing, and the exploration of a 'feminine god' that is outside the grasp of patriarchal religion and theology, but also is 'yet to come'. Irigaray aspires for an ethics of passion through which each sex rejoices in the wonder of the other. Regarding the relationship between sexuality and language, she points out that female sexual pleasure is fundamentally auto-erotic and plural. According to Irigaray, the psychic is never bisexual but always male or female.

Feminist Practice and Poststructuralist Theory is written by Chris Weedon, published by Basil Blackwell Oxford, in 1987. The idea of an essential womanhood common to all women, suppressed or repressed by patriarchy, recurs in Weeden's book as the mark of 'radical-feminist theory'. It is initially listed together with 'socialist-feminist and psychoanalytic feminist theories' as various attempts to systematize individual insights about the oppression of women into relatively coherent theories of patriarchy, inspite of authors' statement that radical-feminist writers are hostile to theory because they see it as a form of male dominance which co-opts women and suppresses the feminine. On page 135 the writer says:

> "For poststructuralist feminism, neither the liberal-feminist attempt to redefine the truth of women's nature within the terms of existing social relations and to establish women's full equality with men, nor the radical-feminist emphasis on fixed difference realized in a separatist context, is politically adequate."[11]

Then the radical-liberal-feminist criticism is the one concerned with 'black and lesbian female experience' appear most clearly in Weedon's eyes as the most extreme in the case of lesbian writing.

Money, Sex and Power, written by Nancy Hartsock and published in 1985, draws on Marxist's analysis of ideology to argue that it is the restriction of woman to the private sphere which accounts for her dominance by the man. This exclusion of women for the public sphere affects the organisation of knowledge, specially in academic disciplines. Therefore, Hartsock argues on Marxist line that only on epistemology rooted in production instead of an exchange can ground a way of knowing that distinguishes reality from false appearances. That is to say Hartsock argues that theories of power which employ the market model of exchange can only assume a community based on domination, i.e. the experiences of men. She then concludes that only women's experiences provide a standpoint which can uncover the real relations of male domination.

Women and Madness: The Critical Phallacy (1975), written by Shoshana Felman, examines the impact that Western dichotomized thinking has had on literary criticism and women. Felman uses Jacques Derrida's analysis of the way that oppositional thinking dominates Western culture. Felmen puts a question. I quote: "But what is a 'woman'? Woman is a 'name'. Woman is consequently a 'definable being'—chained to a 'definition' itself implying a model, a definition commanded by a 'logic' of resemblance."

Whether she is a passive angel or an active monster, in other words, the woman writer feels herself to be literally or figuratively crippled by the debilitating alternatives her culture offers her, and the crippling effects of her conditioning sometimes seem to 'breed', like sentences of death in the bloody shoes she inherits from her literary foremothers.

The title of Alcoff's essay, 'Cultural Feminism Versus Post-Structuralism: The Identity Crisis in Feminist Theory' speaks some of the same problems. It tells about a 'crisis in feminist theory' that may be read not only as a crisis over identity, a metacritical doubt and a dispute among feminists as to the notion of identity, but also as a crisis of identity, of self-definition, implying a theoretical impasse for feminism as a whole. She claims that cultural feminists have not challenged the defining of woman but only that definition given by men and have replaced it with the concept of the essential female. On the other hand, the poststructuralist response has been to reject the possibility of defining woman altogether and to replace "the politics of gender or sexual difference—with a plurality of difference where gender loses its position of significance. Alcoff points out that woman is a position from which a feminist politics can emerge rather than a set of attributes."[12] In becoming feminist for instance, women take up a position, a point of perspective, from which to interpret or reconstruct values and meanings.

In the book *Feminism and Postfeminism*, Kanwar Dinesh Singh studies modern Indian woman poets from the feminist and the postfeminist points of view in order to understand the lives and experiences, the norms and values and the psychodynamics and gender roles of Indian women in the new age. This book talks about poets who have been grouped under two phases—the 'Feminist' phase and the 'postfeminist' phase and who specifically show feminist bias and reaction. The writer also discusses how they portray man, how they respond to love, marriage, sexuality, man-woman ties, and their quests for identity. This book is particularly notable as it elucidates the difference between 'Feminism' and 'Femininity'. I quote, "Feminism is, indeed, a serious attempt to analyze, comprehend and clarify how and why is femininity or the feminine sensibility/ experience/expression different from masculinity or the masculine experience. Feminism brings into perspective the points of difference and contrast that characterize the 'feminine identity' or 'feminine psyche/sensibility' or 'femininity' of woman, which can be studied by taking into account the psychosomatic, social and cultural construction of femininity vis-à-vis masculinity. ...Sex and gender are two distinct terms. 'Sex' is a biological identity while 'gender' is a social construct."[13]

Modernity, Feminism and Women Empowerment on the one hand, dwells upon the contemporary conceptual debate and presents a critique of feminist models and marks out the multiple challenges to feminism, and on the other, it includes the social change discourse, the evolution and enflourishment of the concept of women development and its socio-cultural dimensions within its penetrability. This book endeavours to furnish a panoramic view of the development of women debate, discern and dissect lacunae and loopholes in the rationality of the arguments raised, and finally offers viewpoints to make women development meaningful, satisfying and sustainable in social and cultural sense. It tells, 'Both as a way of thought as well as a movement, feminism is an integral part of movement, feminism is an integral part of modernity.... Feminism is the daughter of modernity and is required to obey all the anti-human, often inconsistent, messages from modernity—its father."[14]

"Thus postmodernism undermines the feminist commitment to women's sense of selfhood, to the reappropriation of women's own history in the name of an emancipated future and to the exercise of radical social criticism which uncovers gender, in all its endless variety and monotonous similarity."[15]

This book contains seventeen essays. Some essays like 'Feminism and Modernity: Concept and Problems', 'Cross-Culural Perceptions of Womanhood: Some Ruminations, Some Ramblings', 'Sex and Gender: Cognitive Analysis', 'Beyond

Beijing: Technology and Women', 'Feminine Worth: A Myth or Reality?' are really worth studying.

Women of Color: Defining the Issues, Hearing the Voices begins with an essay by Nina Manasan, a mixed race woman attempting to make sense of the intersections between race theory and identity politics in the academy. Duncan uses her personal experiences to explore the way racism reinforces heterosexisms to erase or leave out of consideration those whom the dominant society does not want to recognize or acknowledge; the lesbian, gay, and bisexual as well as coloured or mixed in our midst. The essay by Rosetta Haynes shows how race, gender, and sexuality converge with textual experimentation in women's autobiographical writings. I quote from the book:

"Feminism has long been thought of as a single, unitary movement of theory, and, as such, has been accused of being a 'white, middle-class women's movement'. Historically this may have been true, one need to only reread Betty Friedan to see how early radical feminism spoke to a limited audience. Today, however, feminists and others conceptualize feminism in greater varieties, rather than as a unitary monolith."[16]

"Lesbian, gay, and bisexual theorists and film critics search novels, films, and other cultural texts for any indication of lesbian or gay themes, 'the love that dare not speak its name'. For example, Deborah McDowell, Bonnie Zimmerman, and Teresa de Lauretis, to name a few, have attempted to reread familiar narratives for lesbian content, asserting the notion of 'coding' as a significant representational strategy for lesbian and gay texts."[17]

"Feminist phase theory identifies five common phases of thinking about women: male scholarship, compensatory scholarship, bifocal scholarship, feminist scholarship, and multifocal or relational scholarship. Each phase of feminist theory requires an examination of the level of consciousness about the exclusion of women and the steps needed to include women in the major fields or disciplines within the curriculum."[18]

Feminist Theory: The Intellectual Traditions of American Feminism is a teaching book meant to present and interpret the main traditions of feminist theory in the context of their historical and philosophical roots. It provides a convenient and comprehensive summary of the diverse philosophical strains that make up the intellectual heritage of modern feminism. The book is about the American feminist tradition, it includes only those British or European theories that have had a significant influence on American feminism. The various chapters are divided as 'Enlightenment Liberal Feminism', 'Cultural Feminism', 'Feminism and Marxism', 'Feminism and Freudianism', 'Feminism and Existentialism', 'Radical Feminism', 'The New Feminist Moral Vision', 'The Eighties and Beyond' etc. Some of the lines from the book are as follows:

"Perhaps the most radical of the cultural feminist positions developed by Stanton was her critique of religion, in particular Christianity. She was joined in this by Matilda Joslyn Gage whose woman, Church and State remain one of the most powerful pieces of feminist theory produced in the nineteenth century, one that had fallen into obscurity until it was republished in 1980."[19]

"Mackinnon argues that feminist theory may be distinguished from Marxist theory in that feminism must focus on sexuality or gender rather than material conditions"[20]

"The Feminists also attacked love as an 'institution' that promotes vulnerability, dependence, possessiveness, susceptibility to pain, and prevents the full development of woman's human potential."[21]

"There is a way out of this dilemma, it seems, and that is to integrate what it means to be female into what it means to be human. In other words, if women get pregnant, then people get pregnant, and for the law to treat all people equally it must provide for the fact that pregnancy is a human experience. Humans have children; therefore, the law must accommodate itself to the fact that humans have to care for them."[22]

Faces of Feminism has been divided into 4 parts and 13 chapters: The Early Years 1840-1870, The Golden Years 1870-1920, The Intermission 1920-1960, and The Modern Movement. It says that feminism as a social movement has been of less interest than the documentation of and explanation for women's continuing inequality. There is, of course, a very good reason why comparative studies of feminism are so rare, since such a study carries with at the risk of superficiality if not of downright error. The anti-feminism is less easy to define because feminist goals have often been opposed by those who, using my definition, are feminists themselves. Some thoughts from this book are as follows:

"To a large extent, therefore, the effect of the evangelical movement on feminism was to be conservative rather than radical, and even when it led women outside the home it was primarily in order to bring the domestic virtues into the public domain."[23]

"Celibacy was important to the feminists because it attempted to set up an alternative role for women apart from the traditional female sphere of marriage and motherhood: an alternative, indeed, that was followed from choice by many of the pioneers. It enabled them to avoid the sexual and economic subordination of marriage, while at the same time pursuing for themselves an interesting and challenging career."[24]

"If, by the end of the 1920s, the equal rights feminists were no longer dominant within the women's movement, the 1930s accentuated their decline still further so that, as in the United States, feminism became almost synonymous with welfare."[25]

"An important part of the feminist case was the need to free girls from a forced marriage. Economic independence, through educational and employment opportunities and changes in the law of property, was, in effect, the passport that enabled a woman not only to choose not to marry at all but even, under certain circumstances, to leave her husband. The feminists were therefore by no means traditional in their attitude to marriage and divorce."[26]

Women's Writing: Test and Context, a famous book edited by Jasbin Jain (Rawat Publications, Nagpur and New Delhi, 2004), brings together thirty-one essays on women's writing. They focus on the validity of women's writing and traces its contribution to the construction of a female self. It expresses that marginalized as trivial, ghettoised as militant and subversive, opposed to the 'universal' and downgraded as concerned with the victim syndrome, women's writing has finally found a place for itself as voicing the experience of half of humanity. The essays in this volume concern themselves with theoretical issues and historical perspectives, with spatial metaphors and discourse, analysis, with cultural constructs and linguistic textures, with myth and mythologizing and history and dehistoricising. Rebellion, definance, madness, fantasy, and comedy are some of the strategies used by women writers to communicate and get their meaning across.

This is again basically a theory based book. I quote: "Women's writing cannot be treated as a monolithic structure and all women's writing is not necessarily feminist. But women when they write 'think back through their mothers' (Woolf, 93) and their writing has its own characteristics and qualities."[27]

"The feminist critics in postcolonial India have to contend not only against the constructions put upon the 'Indian woman' by the colonial discourse or the Western feminist criticism but also have to wage an even more arduous struggle against the entrenched patriarchal structures in the country which still continue to control and restrict the lives of women in one form or the other."[28]

Feminism: Theory, Criticism, Analysis, written by Sushila Singh, is organized around three approaches towards understanding feminism—theoretical tenets, literary criticism, and applications. Beginning with an account of the nature of feminist movement and mapping out the feminist ideology, the book presents feminist thought and the major concerns of feminist theory in a clear and concise manner, but in its application form its area is limited as it deals with woman in Stanton, Mailor, Margaret Drabble and Joyce Carol Oates. It remains silent as far as Indian fiction in English is concerned. It also explains nothing regarding issues like Lesbian feminism, Eco-feminism, etc. Male's point of view regarding feminism is also absent. But still this book is a torch-bearer for scholars of feminism. I will quote some paragraphs from the book itself:

"The word 'feminism', however, must be understood in its broadest sense as referring to an intense awareness of identity as a woman, and interest in feminine problems. Its meaning should not be restricted to the advocacy of women's rights."[29]

"Feminism originates in the perception that there is something wrong with society's treatment of women. It attempts to analyse the reasons for and dimensions of women's oppression, and to achieve women's liberation. To some, liberation is defined as social equality with men, while others feel that this narrow definition reflects the class bias of what is described variously as bourgeois feminism, career feminism, mainstream feminism or liberal feminism."[30]

"When we use the words 'woman' and 'man' 'female' and 'male', 'feminine' and 'masculine' we are always deploying what we understand as artificial, socially determined signifiers. The changing resonances in meaning affect the lives and art of the writers. Therefore biographical speculations are not irrelevant since the concepts 'female' and 'male' have an impact on human experience which has so far been gendered."[31]

REFERENCES

1. Mary Wollstonecraft, *A Vindication of the Rights of Woman*, Batimore: Penguin, 1975, 145.
2. *Ibid.*, 118.
3. Simone de Beauvoir, *The Second Sex*, translated by H.M. Parshley, Penguin, 1972, written in French, published as *Le Deuxiene Sexe*, in 1949, first published in English by Jonathan Cape in 1953.
4. Sandra Gilbert and Susan Gubar, *The Madwoman in the Attic: The Woman Writer and the Nineteenth Century Literary Imagination*, New Haven: Yale University Press, 1979.
5. Sandra Gilbert and Susan Gubar, *No Man's Land: The Place of Woman Writer in Twentieth Century*, Vol. 1, *The War of the Words*, New Haven: Yale University Press, 1988.
6. Elaine Showalter, *A Criticism of Our Own: Autonomy and Assimilation in Afro-American and Feminist Literary Theory*, New York: Harcourt, 1989.
7. Kate Millett, *Sexual Politics,* New York: Doubleday and Company Inc., 1970, 46.
8. Betty Friedan, *The Feminine Mystique*, 1963.

9. Hélène Cixous, *The Newly Born Woman*, Manchester: Manchester University Press, 1987.
10. Luce Irigaray, *The Sex which is Not One,* Ithaca, NY: Cornwell University Press, 1977, 28.
11. Chris Weedon, *Feminist Practice and Poststructuralist Theory,* Oxford: Basil Blackwell, 1987, 135.
12. Alcoff, *The Politics of Reality: Essays in Feminist Theory,* Trumansburg, NY: The Crossing Press, 1983, 434-435.
13. Kanwar Dinesh Singh, *Feminism and Postfeminism*, New Delhi: Sarup and Sons, 2004, 3.
14. Abha Awasthi and A.K. Srivastava (eds.), *Modernity, Feminism and Women Empowerment*, Jaipur and New Delhi: Rawat Publications, 2001, 11-12.
15. *Ibid.*, 13-14.
16. Diane Leng Hoeveur and Janet K. Boles, *Women of Color: Defining the Issues, Hearing the Voices,* London: Green Wood Press, 2001, 15.
17. *Ibid.*, 28.
18. *Ibid.,* 179.
19. Josephine Downvan, *Feminist Theory: The Intellectual Traditions of American Feminism,* New York: The Continuum Publishing Company, 1996, 36.
20. *Ibid.*, 20.
21. *Ibid.*, 143.
22. *Ibid.*, 146.
23. Olive Banus, *Faces of Feminism,* New York: St. Martin's Press, 1981, 26.
24. *Ibid.*, 97.
25. *Ibid.*, 171-172.
26. *Ibid.*, 146.
27. Jasbir Jain (ed.), *Women's Writing: Text and Context,* Nagpur and New Delhi: Rawat Publications, 2004, 7.
28. *Ibid.*, 23-24.
29. Sushila Singh, *Feminism: Theory, Criticism, Analysis,* Delhi: Pencraft International, 2004, 21.
30. *Ibid.*, 30.
31. *Ibid.*, 31.

10 A Brief Historical Survey of Feminism: A Global Scenario

To understand the future of women, we must appreciate the history of feminism that has brought us to this revolutionary moment. In the past two centuries, revolution has transformed women's lives. Feminist politics originated where capitalism, industrial growth, democratic theory, and socialist critiques conveyed, as they did in Europe and North America after 1800. Women and their male allies began to agitate for equal educational, economic, and political opportunities, a struggle that continues to the present. By 1900 an international women's movement advanced these goals in urban areas of Latin America, the Middle East, and Asia. Since 1970 feminism has spread globally, in both industrialized nations and in the developing regions too.

Given their specific historical origins, the feminist politics initially forged in Europe and North America have not simply expanded throughout the world. Elsewhere, abundant forms of women's resistance to men's patriarchal authority predated Western democratic theories; they continue to influence feminist movements today. Both the term feminism and the politics it represents, have been continually transformed by the evolving responses of women and men from a variety of cultures. Indeed, women's politics have developed organically in settings so diverse that the plural feminisms more accurately describes them.

By the year 2000 these growing international movements to improve women's lives increasingly influenced each other, due in part to the forum provided by the United Nations Decade for women from 1975 to 1985 and the follow-up conference in Beijing in 1995. While they share the conviction that women deserve full human rights, international feminism often diverge in their emphasis. Only some concentrate solely on women while others recognize complex links to the politics of race, class, religion and nationality. Despite these differences, most Western feminists have learned that global economic and political justice are prerequisites to securing women's rights. Women in the developing world have found that transnational feminist movement can help establish strategic international support for their efforts at home.

None of these feminist movements has proceeded without opposition, including formidable backlash in every era in which women have gained public authority. Nonetheless, at the beginning of the twenty-first century, the historical conditions that promote feminism can be found in different parts of the world.

First coined in France in the 1880 as féminism, it spread through European countries in the 1890s and to North and South America by 1910. Western women's movements also significantly expanded their agendas after 1960s. Along with demands for economic and political rights, women's liberation revived a politics of difference through its critique of interpersonal relations. Since the 1970s women's bookstores have served a growing audience of readers in search of new images to support their politics. The growth of bookstores and publishers, along with art galleries, museum exhibitions, and concerts featuring the creative works of women, parallels the reclamation of the body as a means of feminist empowerment. Women's creativity encompasses strategies based on both female difference and human equality. Feminist artists launched their own alternative cultural spaces and demanded access to institutions that previously excluded them; the theater, the museum, the concert hall. Once admitted to these public cultural spaces, feminists bring to their arts not only an exploration of women's experiences, such as motherhood and sexual violence, but also the complex politics of race, nationality, and sexuality.

Vietnamese and **Cambodians** struggle with legacies of decades of war and women of both countries face daunting political, economic, and social realities. Women of Vietnam experience rural poverty, ecological and health damage and a double burden of outside jobs and domestic work. Unlike women in Vietnam, Cambodian women struggle with high rates of illiteracy and clear wage discrimination. There is a growing problem of trafficking of women and girls in Cambodia.

Women have legal equality under the Constitution, and the state continues to draft laws ensuring the protection of women's rights. However, women are still not adequately represented in the economic and political structures of the country. Gender equality within the family is not a reality for most women; those with responsible positions are often still seen as naturally better suited for child care and domestic work. The image of the nurturing mother can be a figure of social and political agency, or, with increasing privatization, a woman who accepts a double burden without complaint. As a result of the struggles of women's organisations working in coalition in the early 1990s, Cambodia'a Constitution now has progressive legal provisions regarding the rights of women. The National Assembly has drafted laws such as the Law on Abortion, the Law on Domestic Violence, and the Law on Trafficking, which further protect women. However, implementation and enforcement are problematic. Courts tend to favour men in judgments and with a higher level of illiteracy women are less likely to know the law and are more easily intimidated. Female representation in the weak judicial system is low; out of 110 judges in Cambodia only eight are women; of forty prosecutors, none are women. Cambodian women also face discrimination in education and employment, and they are poorly represented in political and economic structures, inspite of the fact that traditionally women enjoy a relatively high social status. Thus, such circumstances pave way to feminist revolt and movements.

Feminists in **Serbia** and **Croatia** have worked on peace activism and solidarity among women and founded anti-war and feminist movements to resist nationalism, sexism and war. There is little education available on birth control and pregnancy which is a constant fear for woman. In some cases women are also resorting to prostitution to feed themselves and their children. In 1986, feminists in **Belgrade** defined their organisation 'women and society' as feminist. They held workshops and public discussions on violence, abortion, sexuality, worker's rights, psychiatry and medicine. Feminist organisations have supported democratisation in Yugoslavia.

Women in Black made its first appearance in **Belgrade** on 9th October 1991. The founders of the feminist anti-violence movement in Serbia, view violence against women and children as a social and political issue, not as the private interactions between men and women, or within the family. Women's groups that have formed to resist war and violence bring a feminist analysis to Serbian nationalism and men's violence against women. Feminist groups in Belgrade point out that both private and state violence stem from patriarchy. Patriarchy considers that men's violence in their family is a private family matter and their ideology of privacy permits violence in all other domains of society.

The women in **Sudan** from the North and the South, decided to come together to fight for peace, democracy, social justice, human rights and women's equal rights, through their women's organisation and the Sudanese Women's voice for peace. It was experienced that immediately after seizing power in 1989, the NIF regime dismissed most women judges, diplomats, army and female police officers, and women who held high posts in the civil service. They banned the Union and all the other women's organisations, except the NIF women's organisation. They issued new family laws, which deprived women, as wives, mothers, and daughters, of their rights. For instance, these laws give the father the right to stop and dissolve his daughter's marriage if she does not agree with the arrangement, irrespective of her wishes and choices. They made it compulsory for working women and female students to tie their hair and wear a long dress or trousers under the roab, or else, be dismissed.

For all this, women are fighting against the regime and at the same time putting pressure on the opposition to represent women in their organisation. Despite difficulties and suffering, they are sure they will succeed in the end.

The **Korea** women's Hotline, started in 1983, focuses on domestic violence. It established the first shelter for battered women in Korea and in recent years has addressed the issue of militarized prostitution. In the Philippines, several women's activity organisations are dealing with the long-term fallout from the U.S. basis. The centre offered night-care services for children of bar women, temporary shelter, counseling, referrals and other crisis interventions. Fifty-five women activists from Korea, Okinawa, Mainland, Japan, the Philippines, and the United States gathered in Washington, D.C. (8-13 October, 1998) for the second international meeting of the East Asia, U.S. Women's Network. They argue that eliminating gender inequalities, and specifically ending violence against women, must be a fundamental element of a demilitarized future. The U.S. military system also harms women in the military, many of whom experience sexual harassment and women and children in military families where domestic violence is much higher than in civilian families. Women in the U.S. need to work with women from East Asia and many other countries to redefine security.

Iranian women kept pace with the progress of the movement, and were present in every area. To shatter the notion of male superiority, which bound the hands and feet of Iranian men and women, they voluntarily ended their marriages in divorce so that no one had any responsibility to anyone or anything but the fallout was on the Khomeini regime. Their women chose to take this world defined as being a woman, the weaker sex, and to disengage themselves from their traditional role, in which, to be recognised, they required the existence of a husband. In the same fashion feminists' notion was to insist that men had to recognise their wives' right to choose between a life of resistance and a private life. They had to learn to look upon women not as women, but as equal human beings.

Traditionally, **Tibetan** women enjoyed a higher social status than their counterparts in many other Asian societies. They were not subject to foot binding, arranged marriages or a one-child policy. But even in Tibet, it was a belief that to achieve *nirvana*, it was necessary to be male; thus women prayer goes: "May I reject a feminine body and be reborn a male one."

Most recently, the Tibetan and American women involved in the movement have focused their work on testifying to the United Nations about the forced sterilization and torture of Tibetan women. But Tibetan women have developed non-violent action and ritual. They present a major force in history through the power of non-violent actions combined with their deep spirituality that infuses every movement of their lives.

Post-Liberation women in **Eritrea** has something special for the world to look at. Among other visionary areas for women in the National Democratic Programme of the EPLF was the special section on 'Women's Rights'. Feminists over there asserted for the development of a national women's union, freedom from domestic confinement, the promulgation of equitable marriage and family laws, equality to men in politics, economics and social life, equal pay for equal work and parental leave, provision for child care and kindergartens, a stipulation to protect women workers from harmful work, leadership development and the eradication of prostitution. Among the most impressive social emancipatory documents, manuals and events for women were the EPLF marriage laws and the various training seminars on life and marriage offered to both men and women in the field. There is little doubt that the NUEW has played a major role inforcing the issue of the emancipation of women to the forefront of the struggle. EPLF women fighters had begun the gender image-building in a positive way, they saw themselves, and were seen by others, as among the political and educated elites in the towns, as models of emancipated women, women fighters as heroes from a familiar icon in post-liberation Eritrea.

In **France** the relational feminism led to the seemingly paradoxical doctrine of 'equality in difference'. The French theorists argued that equity is distinct from equality. The basic tenets were that there were both biological and cultural distinctions between the sexes, a concept of womanly or manly nature, of a sharply defined sexual division of laborer, or roles in the family and society.

The Anglo-American feminist tradition, however, advocated the individualist through as the only 'politically correct' form till as recently as 1970s. This strand placed political priority on enactment of the Equal Rights Amendment and on demolishing the gender stratified educational system and economy that disadvantaged women through occupational segregation.

The earliest efforts to create an international women's movement offers reproduced colonial relations. Just as women of colour within the United States challenged white feminists to recognize their racial biases, so too women from Asia, Africa, and the Middle East took issue with what scholars later termed 'feminist orientalism', the tendency to view all women outside the West as exotic, sexuality oppressed others. At an international conference in 1935 Shareefeh Hamid Ali of India spoke for women 'of the East'. At the NGO forums women did debate international politics as well as economic development policies. Western feminists arrived with a focus on equal rights to education, property, and political authority. For women from Asia, Africa and Latin America, however, rural and urban poverty represented the most pressing challenges to human rights. 'To talk feminism to a woman who has no water, no food and no home is to talk nonsense'—became India's diction.

The exchanges at the official UN conference and the unofficial NGO meetings proved highly educational for Western feminists. Delegates learned about the daily problems that confronted women globally living under apartheid in South Africa, struggling for self-determination in Palestine, bringing water, sewers and electricity to poor Brazilian women trying to feed families throughout the world.

The NGO gatherings especially convinced many Western women that world poverty and national liberation were feminist issues because they affected women's lives around the globe. Just as women of colour in the United States built their own feminist support structure, Latin American, African, and Asian women met to define their feminist agendas. A feminist dilemma concerning the controversial notion of a 'unified sisterhood' presumed the relevance of Western politics to the rest of the world regardless of local conditions. In Amrit Basu's terms, the challenge of local feminisms complicates sisterhood. Just as women of colour in the West testified about their racially specific identities, women outside the West have explained why gender cannot be the sole determinant of their politics. Peasant and working class women in Africa, Asia and Latin America have been adamant that for them, economic justice, along with cultural and national sovereignty, must become a priority of feminism. In contrast to European and North American drives for individual rights, these local activists often stress women's domestic identities.

The transnational approach has enabled more activists from a range of cultures to embrace feminism as a political identity. When the women's league of the African National Congress returned from exile in 1990, they proclaimed that 'feminism has been misinterpreted in most third world countries—there is nothing writing with feminism.' It is as progressive or reactionary as nationalism. With the establishment of a democratic government, they dropped their call for 'liberation before feminism' and began to negotiate for equal representation of women in the ANC.

In the West, liberal feminism called for the extension of men's individual rights to women, socialism concentrated on organizing women as wage labourers, and radical feminism emphasized the power relations between men and women in familial and personal relationships. The expansion of feminism internationally makes even clearer why all of these political streams must converge.

Acknowledging the interconnections of women's rights, economic justice, and world politics, United Nations Secretary-General Boutros Boutros-Ghal opened the 1995 UN sponsored Fourth World Conference on Women in Bejing by declaring that the 'great political project of the twentieth century', was to secure equality for women and men, in reality as well as in law. The global stage had expanded to include the voices of women whose politics of location, both geographic and personal strengthened the feminist movement.

11 Contemporary Criticism of Feminism

Criticism of feminism is a whole ideology. Criticism of specific types of feminism and criticism of specific feminist ideas have come from feminists themselves, along with non-feminists, masculists, social conservatives, and social progressives.

Post-colonial feminists criticise certain ideas of Western forms of feminism, notably radical feminism and its most basic assumption, universalisation of the female experience. They argue that these assumptions cannot so easily be applied to women for whom gender oppression comes second to, for example, racial or class oppression. From the perspective of some strands of feminism, as well as the 'men's movement' and 'queer theory', inequalities and stereotypes based on gender are detrimental to both men and women and both sexes suffer from the expectations of traditional gender roles.

Many who support 'masculism' argue that because of both traditional gender roles and sexism infused into society by feminists, males are and have been oppressed. Marriage Rights advocates, oppose feminist aspirations to replace the traditional family, as illustrated by statements made by a variety of feminist leaders such as Shelia Croman's view that marriage constitutes slavery for women, and the women's movement must concentrate on attacking this institution and that freedom for women cannot be won without the abolition of marriage. Men and family rights groups oppose feminists such as Robin Morgan, the openly lesbian editor of *Ms. Magazine*, who advocated 'man-hating' as an honourable and viable political act and concludes that the inequities between men and women cannot be resolved until marriage is destroyed. They are also critical of feminist encouragement of lesbian agendas which undermine the traditional role of men in the family such as Sheila Cronan's *National 'Now Times'* (January 1988) interviews, statements declaring every woman must be willing to be identified as a lesbian to be fully feminist. Many critics of feminism are alarmed by the prevalence of lesbians such as Patricia Ireland, the head of NOW, in feminist leadership roles. Men's Rights advocates view much of contemporary feminist issues 'extremist' due to their perception that feminist demands such as equal rights has been achieved. Issues such as Violence Against Woman Act are viewed as discriminating of man. Father's Rights advocates are critical of feminist efforts to block shared parenting, or joint custody, after divorce.

Masculism, also known as masculinism, is a number of ideologies found in the streams of the men's movement. It is the male equivalent of feminism. Masculism is viewed by its proponents as being an egalitarian view of gender issues, with the focus on men's experience. However, masculism is not merely a response to feminism. Although many masculist ideas serve as a rejoinder to feminist views, there are many issues, such as military conscription and fatherhood, that have been identified as concerns for men in their own right. Warren Farrell is probably the most prominent author using the term 'masculist' today. Terry Daly is claimed to have been the first to use it in print.

Masculism is a movement and an ideology that considers the sexes complementary and interdependent by necessity; masculists generally believe that the expression of differentiated sex roles is natural and should be exempted from government interference. This contrasts with how these masculists view feminist ideology. Masculism is the ideological flip side of feminism. This term 'Masculism' itself did not gain currency until the end of the 20th century. While some feminists consider the sexes as having the same capacities in virtually every respect, they denounce differentiated sex roles as an oppressive artificial construct, many masculists believe, on the contrary, that profound sex differences are inherent in human nature, and that feminists who have attempted to negate these differences by legislation and social engineering are dragging civilization through a fallacious experiment. Some masculists further state that sexual equality laws have resulted in making feminist ideology, as they see it, as mainstream that such laws serve primarily women and have created significant unconstitutioned discrimination against men. While in their view, most feminism rails against an all-powerful patriarchy, many masculists consider patriarchy 'inevitable'. Some believe that feminism has achieved a covert matriarchy by means of such device. They also complain that feminist ideology is taught in universities, where it is misleadingly labeled as 'women's studies'. The term 'masculism' may be used interchangeably with 'men's rights movement', but conservatism in the men's rights movement often reserve the term 'masculism' for the liberal broach of the movement. The essence of the division between liberal and conservative anti-feminists is secularism versus religion. Leftist masculists are fond of pointing out in this regard that the same conflict existed in feminism until the past few decades when the patriarchal women of the Right were converted to feminism. Masculism is simply an attempt to counter ideology with ideology and in that manner create a 'New Patriarchy'. There is no conflict in goals, only the usual Left-Right dynamics.

There exists an alternate view of masculism as a complementary movement to feminism. In this viewpoint, both feminism and masculism are attempts to correct disadvantages induced by gender roles—feminism addresses areas where women are seen to be disadvantaged (pay, promotion etc.) while masculism addresses areas where men are disadvantaged (criminal prosecution and sentencing, etc.). Masculists with this view may object to specific aspects of feminism, or to the expressed views of specific self-defined feminist groups, but do not reject feminism as a concept, or believe that the feminist movement as a whole is inimical to masculism. However, it should be noted that many masculists vehemently decry this idea, and do not believe that masculism and feminism can possibly co-exist. Finally the definition of masculism by Tom Smith explains the real concept. It says, "Masculism is a men's movement ideology that advocates for the abolition of political and cultural assumptions of equality between sexes. A realistic approach to sex differences is that attempts to identify those differences and how they are best expressed in the social and political milieu. It supports the establishment of a modern patriarchy and assumes that we are now living in a matriarchy."[1]

REFERENCE

1. Tom Smith (OIM) (oim@yahoo.com)

12 Don't Call Me A Feminist

Finding a feminist may be a hard task these days. Feminists are tagged as hating just about everyone and everything—but most of all, feminists hate men. The tragic point is that while many of today's men understand the need for equality between genders, many men refuse to associate themselves with feminism. Ask them what they think of feminists, and you may hear a string of negative associations: radical, man-hating, bra-burning, and worse. Women may be acceptable as equals, but feminists are often seen as frightening, threatening, or simply unnecessary. This is applicable on women as well. The recurrent caricatures of feminists reveal an anxiety that feminism is somehow antithetical to femininity, that to embrace its politics is to reject a gender identity that many woman and men wish to preserve.

This hostility to feminists and feminism cannot be dismissed simply by avoiding the terms, for these harsh stereotypes can always be used to discredit women activists, whether they call themselves feminists or not. Even in Indian scenario most of the very popular Indian-English novelists are not ready to be labeled as feminists. They are constantly working for the upliftment of the female folk by voicing their unheard sentiments, and by peeping into their inner psyche.

Even then they proclaim 'Don't call me a Feminist'. The term 'feminist' has been handled rather cautiously by many women writers. They consider even the term 'women writer' as derogatory, taking away their artistic autonomy and identity and categorizing them by gender. In a paper presented at a seminar, 'The Dilemma of the Women Writers', Shashi

Deshpande protested: "It is a curious fact that serious writing by women is invariably regarded as feminist writing. A woman who writes of women's experiences often brings in some aspects of those experiences that have angered her, caused her strong feelings, I don't see why this has to be labelled feminist fiction."[1]

In an interview with Vanamala Viswanatha, she said that she does not "believe in having a propagandist or sexist purpose to my (her) writing. If it presents such a perspective, it is only a coincidence."[2]

Anita Desai has expressed the same reservations. In an interview with Yashodhara Dalmia she said, "I find it impossible to whip up any interest in a mass of women marching forward under the banner of feminism."[3]

What writers are wary about are the political and ideological implications behind the term. Even those women writers who are living and writing in a world in which feminism is a force that cannot be avoided.

Even the most modern, prolific and bold writer Shobha Dé once stated that she preferred not to be branded as a feminist. To quote her:

> "I write with a great deal of empathy towards women. Without raising a feminist flag, I feel very strongly about the woman's situation"[4]

Anybody can be surprised to hear these words from a woman who appears to uphold liberated views about emancipated women. Her novels are deeply rooted in this firm conviction of the novelist.

The media have contributed to this discomfort by treating feminism as a thing of the past. In the United States, for example, ever since its revival in the 1960s journalists have proclaimed the death of feminism. In 1976 Harper declared a 'requiem for the women's movement', in 1980 the *New York Times* assured readers that the 'radical days of feminism are gone', in 1990 *Newsweek* trumpeted 'the failure of feminism'. Unconvinced by two decades of obituaries, in 1998 *Time* asked readers to respond online to the question 'Is feminism dead?' So ubiquitous is this story that a feminist journalist recently labeled it 'False Feminist Death Syndrome'. Perhaps these writers notice feminism only during periods of mass public protest and overlook its quieter but more pervasive forms. Or perhaps they are engaging in a form of wishful thinking, for given the power of the media, declaring the death of feminism could become a self-fulfilling prophecy.

If feminism, as I will argue, is so deeply rooted historically and so expansive in the present, why the contradictory claims in the press that it is near death? Why is feminism highly unpopular, even vilified, when first articulated? I suspect that the answers to these questions lie in part in what might be called 'fear of feminism'. No matter how insightful its politics, feminism feels deeply threatening to many people, both women and men. By providing a powerful critique to the idea of a timeless social hierarchy, in which God or nature preordained women's dependence on men, feminism exposes the historical construction, and potential deconstruction, of categories such as gender, race, and sexuality. Fear that feminism will unleash changes in familiar family, sexual and racial relationships can produce anti-feminist politics among those who wish to conserve older forms of social hierarchy. Not all participants will claim the label feminist, though many activists would like them to. When women in her native Dominican Republic 'Shake their heads disapprovingly and say, 'yo no soy feminista, pero, si, creo ...." (I am not a feminist, but I believe ....), novelist Julia Alvarez feels 'that by refusing to claim their feminism openly these women make the burden all the harder for the rest of us who are willing to pay the price. Yet those who still fear feminism as a political identity are living and breathing its politics whenever they stand up for themselves, their families, their rights.

Those who do not oppose change may still fear certain connotations of feminism. Neither is a very pleasant prospect, especially if feminism is presented in the oversimplified language of male oppression and female of victimization. Portraying a movement as blaming one group (white men) and denying the resilience of another (all women) will keep it unpopular, even though, as I will argue, feminism at its best offers much more complex interpretations of the dynamics of gender, race, and power.

In the past forty years feminism has greatly expanded the space for women artists, yet not all or many women artists consider themselves feminists. For some writing must have no sex or gender, lest the particularities of identity limit the subject-matter of the artist calling attention to female difference still provokes fear of exclusion. However, many artists have come to acknowledge that by being labeled as feminists their sphere will be limited. But this is not completely true. There are authors like South African writer Lindiwe Mabuza who counters this thought process and says boldly, "If feminism means recognition of my fullest capacities, welcome feminism. If it means starving off the hand that wants to destroy me, I say all power to feminism. If I can fight for myself and my like than I proudly call myself 'A Feminist'.[5]

REFERENCES

1. Shashi Deshpande, "The Dilemina of the Woman Writes," *Woman in Fiction and Fiction by Women*, Eds. C.D. Narasimhaiah and C.N. Srinath, Mysore: Dhvanyaloka, 33.
2. Shashi Deshpande, "A Woman's World ..... All the Way," Interview by Vanamala Vishwanatha, *Literature Alive*, 1-3 (1987), 14.
3. Anita Desai, "Interview with Anita Desai" by Yashodhara Dalmia, *The Times of India*, 29 April 1979.
4. Shobha Dé: *The Hindustan Times Magazine*, 12th February 1995, 3.
5. Quoted in Lindiwe Mabuze and Elaine Maria Upton, "Born to Struggle," *Learning to Write: An Interview with Lindiwe Mabuza in Feminist Studies*, 21: 3, 1995, 625.

13 Feminist Jurisprudence: An Overview

Feminist jurisprudence is a philosophy of law based on the political, economic and social equality of sexes. As a field of legal scholarship, feminist jurisprudence began in 1960s. It holds a new significant place in U.S. Law and legal thought and influence many debates on sexual and domestic violence, inequality in the workplace, and gender based discrimination. Through various approaches feminists have identified gendered components and gendered implications of seemingly neutral laws and practices. Laws affecting employment, divorce, and sexual harassment, have all benefited from the analysis and insight of feminist jurisprudence.

Feminists believe that history was written from a male point of view and does not reflect women's role in making history and structuring society. Male-written history has created a bias in the concepts of human nature, gender potential, and social arrangements. The language, logic, and structure of the law are male created and reinforce male values. By presenting male's characteristics as a 'norm' and females characteristics as deviation from the 'normal', the prevailing conceptions of law reinforce and perpetuate patriarchal power. Feminists challenge the belief that the biological make-up of men and women is so different that certain behaviour can be attributed on the basis of sex; gender, feminists say, is created socially, not biologically. Sex determines such matters as physical appearance and reproductive capacity, but not psychological, moral or social tracts.

Though feminists share commitments to equality between men and women, feminist jurisprudence is not uniform. There are three major schools of thought within feminist jurisprudence. Traditional or liberal feminism asserts that women are just as rational as men and therefore should have equal opportunity to make their own choices. Liberal feminists challenge the assumption of male authority and seek to erase gender-based distinctions recognised by law, thus enabling women to compete in the marketplace.

Another school of feminist legal thought, cultural feminists, focuses on the differences between men and women and celebrates those differences. Following the research of psychologist Card Gilligan, this group of thinkers asserts that women emphasize the importance of relationships, contexts and reconciliation of conflicting interpersonal positions, whereas men emphasize abstract principles of rights and logic. The goal of this school is to give equal recognition to women's moral voice of caring and communal values.

Like the Liberal feminist school of thought, Radical or Dominant feminism focuses on inequality. It asserts that men, as a class, have dominated women as a class, creating gender inequality. For radical feminists gender is a question of power. Radical feminists urge us to abandon traditional approaches that take maleness as their reference point. They argue that sexual equality must be constructed on the basis of women's difference from man and not be a mere accommodation of that difference. In a feminist jurisprudence, the burden of proof would shift toward recognition of the present gender inequalities—taking into account the particular details of sexual inequalities, statistical disparities, and the degree to which statutes work toward an end to male supremacy.

Today European and North American feminists defend reproductive choice, while African feminists seek to eliminate female genital cutting and Indian feminists target dowry deaths, rape and domestic violence. In each case achieving legal reform represents only one step in the process of changing long standing attitudes about women's maternal, domestic and sexual lives.

14 The New Woman

Although during the early years of the twentieth century the attention of the feminists was upon the campaign for women's suffrage and its consequences, a much greater impact was being made upon women's lives by changes that had little directly to do with the feminist movement and that involved, in both India and Black America, a loosening of manners and morals and an emancipation, for the young middle-class girl in particular, from those suffocating conventions that had restricted her within the narrow world of morality. These changes did not, of course, occur suddenly. By the twin of the century, however, the most rigid of the restrictions had gone, even if some irksome restraints still remained. A study of the treatment of sex in marital education literature shows that during the twentieth century the idea that sex was acceptable only for procreation steadily declined and there was a growing emphasis on the need for mutual sexual satisfaction. The older generation of feminists, however, did not look approvingly at the growing sexual permissiveness. Many feminists saw female sexuality as a trap to keep women pregnant and domesticated, but instead of anticipating a time when woman would be free to enjoy her sexuality she looked forward to a society, where other would lay less emphasis on sex. Thinking along similar lines to Gilman, some argued that men's control over women had turned them into sex slaves with the result that not only men but women too had become oversexualized. The great majority of the feminists at this time condemned both birth control and abortion, while divorce law reform remained an area of great controversy that many feminist preferred to ignore. In 1911 a new feminist journal *The Freewoman* was founded that was committed to the new morality, and opposed the Puritanism. The argument for birth control—like that for family allowances, with which it was, indeed, frequently linked—could also be used to sustain rather than challenge woman's traditional role, by emphasizing and even idealizing her maternal nature. Women believed that they had a right to their own intellectual development. At the same time they could not deny that marriage and maternity were a woman's chief goal in life. Moreover, Indian feminists were of the opinion that a woman's body was essentially her own, they disapproved of pre-marital sex, abortion, masturbation and lesbianism.

The concept of 'free love' was therefore used by these feminists (West) as a personal and individual response to the social and legal constraints that a conventional marriage laid upon them. By remaining free, they hoped to retain not only their independence but those rights that, in spite of some change in the law, they still lost on marriage, including rights over the custody of their children.

Currently, it is politically trendy for even pro-women activists to say that the feminist debate is past its sell date. In a world of globalised capitalism, our new woman is a super creature, who has shattered the glass ceiling. Education and job have offered her equal opportunity and status to choose a life she wants, travel the world and satisfy her desires. She has come a long way. In a developing nation, the glamorous and rich woman is a symbol of achievement of all things, material that men aspire and attain. Besides, it is great to celebrate women, their beauty and their sheen. The 'new woman' today challenges the traditional notions of 'Angel in the house' and 'sexually voracious' image. The 'new woman' is essentially a woman of awareness and consciousness of her low position in the family and society and tries to improve it. The feminist literary criticism has developed as a component of women's movement and its impact has brought about a revolution in literary studies. The emerging 'new woman' is contemplative about her predicament and chooses to protest and fight against the general, accepted norms and currents. What is new and different about these women is that they are prepared to face the consequences of their choices. Their protest is not for equality only but for the right to be acknowledged as individuals—capable of intelligence and feeling. They do not look for freedom outside the house but within too, without painting their lives in various artificial shades of sentiments. This 'new woman' may not be 'ideal' or the 'best' woman. She is new in the dimension of time by being a rebel against the general current of the patriarchal society, and in exploring her true potential, along with the struggle to fulfil her urges and needs. She has carved a niche for herself in almost every area. Today the women movement has assumed an individualistic nature where women demand human rights and personal independence dismissing the erstwhile socially defined roles. However, this does not imply that women today wish to disturb the existing social and economic parameters. They are aware of their exploitation, conscious of their rights and willingly though assertively compromise with situations. Contemporary 'new-woman' is necessarily pro-woman but not entirely anti-man. Her concrete step moves towards better human relationships. Feminists and women writers have caught the new women in this flux and have portrayed them realistically both psychologically as well as physically in their works of art. Such literature has certainly contributed to a fresh exploration of the role and status of women in the contemporary Indian society.

Thus the Indian woman, as appropriately presented in the modern and postmodern fiction written in English by Indian women novelists, behaves unlike her Western counterpart in her evolution from the 'feminine' to the 'female'. She is progressive and conscious of her rights like the contemporary Western counterpart, but she quickly compromises to the fact that a woman's real position lies within the family-unit with her male-counterpart, which she must sustain and protect and not ignore or neglect due to the false notion of being 'liberated'. Simone de Beauvoir said in *The Second Sex*,

> "It is not regard for the opinion of others alone that leads her to give time and care to her appearance and her

> housekeeping. She wants to retain her womanliness for her own satisfaction. She can regard herself with approval throughout her present and past only in combining the life she has made for herself with the destiny that her mother, her childhood games, and her adolescent fantasies prepared for her .... Her mother and her older sisters have inculcated the liking for a nest: a home, an 'interior', of her own. That has always been basic in her dreams of independence. She has no intention of discarding them when she has found liberty by other roads"[1] (694-95)

She further says: "Today the woman who works is less neglectful of her femininity than formerly, and she does not lose her sexual attractiveness. This success, though already indicating progress towards equilibrium, is not yet complete."[2] (695)

Through her efforts she has provided a vast collection of outpourings from the unheard voices of women. Literature not only reveal the trauma of the depressed and wronged women but also make it known to all and sundry that women are now determined to fight for their rights. The women writers in their own voice clearly proclaim and assert that they are women of substance, not merely sex objects or sacrificing persons in the family. And above all, they have established and declared in their own voice that they too are human beings.

The voice of new woman is voiced by Shange Ntozana. I quote:

> "I am space and winds
> like a soft rain or a torrent of dust
> i can move
> be free in time
> a movement is mine always
> i am not like a flower at all
> i can bloom and be a wisp of sunlight
> i'm a rusting of dead leaves and so familiar with tears
> alla this is mine
> so long as i breathe
> i'm gonna dance for all of us
> everybody dead/everybody busy

everybody too burdened to jump
thru a nite a hot and bluesy jump
in the guts of ourselves a dance
is like a dream
i can always remember make it/come again ...
i can make it come again."[3]

REFERENCES

1. Simone de Beauvoir, *The Second Sex*, New York: Penguin Books, First Printed (1949) translated (1984), 694-695.
2. *Ibid.*
3. Shange Ntozana, *Three Pieces*, New York: St. Martin's Press, 1981, 77.

15

Mothering: A Feminist Concern

Motherhood has a history, it has an ideology, it is more fundamental than tribalism or nationalism. The debate over mothering continues to rage inside and outside the feminist community. There are two groups of feminists on this particular issue of mothering. Jeffner Allen argues that giving birth to children buttresses the patriarchy, saps women's energy, and is evolutionarily unsound. She urges women to 'evacuate' mothering. Others like Luce Irigaray have valorized women's childbearing as one of the few expressions of power women under patriarchy possess. These feminists 'embrace motherhood' and decry the loss of female control over the spiritual and physical dimensions of childbirth. Irigaray further holds the view that motherhood is allowed only a small space, denied economic or social status and separated from the very aspect of sexuality. Creativity is a male domain, motherhood is restricted to the nurture and care of the child. The daughter in the patriarchal system must separate from the mother in order to gain her own identity. The daughter is thus 'exiled' from her first identity and history. Irigaray argues that this condition must be rectified by the invention of a new language that redefines motherhood in explicitly sexual terms. Such a language will allow the mother and daughter separate identities but retain their bond.

French Feminist theory in particular has tended to focus on the power of the mother; but this power is not the patriarchal power of dominance and control, but of nurturance and creation. Emancipation from (patriarchy), they claim, requires the liberation of the mother and the revaluing of women's bodily experiences of creation and of women's relationship with women. Finally, a compromise was sought or held by some. It defends that child rearing, if not bearing, must be shared by men and women. The role of mothering is one of nurturing and of caretaking; in the sense, almost anyone can mother.

Webster Dictionary defines mothering as 'caring for another with maternal affection or tenderness'. The concept of motherhood conceived by male imagination restricts woman's quest for wholeness. Motherhood is equated with mother earth; one who should surrender, serve and remain perpetually crushed. Motherhood gains strength; ideologically, from the elevated myth of Mother Goddess but in all practicality, it demands the sacrifice of all ambitions, liberty and identity for the sake of a happy family life. Like maternalists of the early women's movement, contemporary women draw on their identities as mothers to protect the interests of their families. Historian Temma Kaplan has called such maternal authority 'female consciousness' to distinguish it from feminist consciousness. When women act in the name of their assigned gender identity to improve their lives and protect their families, they do not necessarily demand privileges enjoyed by men. Famous American Political Scientist Maxine Molyneux applies the label 'practical gender interest' to describe the agenda of those who accept gender hierarchy but attempt to solve specific problems by making moral claims as mothers.

Feminist and womanist writers have learnt to handle the problem efficiently. The strong feminists believe in the offensive methods and like Alice Walker's Meridian reject all metaphorical and factual concepts of motherhood. Womanist writers (wild approach) on the other hand manipulate the delicate issue intelligently and inscribe a story that narrates the tale of the mother and the woman authentically. It is a common thinking that women will always mother. They know that even if they are working, the well being of their children often requires reciprocal help with babysitting and childcare. Motherhood is a very important part of the role image of many Black women. They grow up with models of mothers, grandmothers, and aunts who have served both roles in their families. Mostly Black women place an extremely high value on motherhood, no matter, how problematic their early years may have been or how much they value the need to raise children. Particularly meaningful and recurrent even in the autobiographies of Black women is their concept of motherhood. It is seldom a monolithic view, easily categorized under a single, stereotypic label. Instead, Black women who focus on this aspect of their lives are more concerned with the multidimensional response of Black women to the honorific yet restrictive place motherhood assumes in life and in literature. Against a background of racial and sexual myths, stablizer for the community, matriarch-Black women autobiographers consistently expand motherhood into a creative and personally fulfilling role. In the autobiographies of Black women, motherhood is a non-individualistic, cultural force that is not based solely on procreation, breeding, or providing numbers.

The Black mother's knowledge and endurance of America's racial hostility and violence are envisioned as strengthening and motivating tools with which she prepares others of her race for self-sufficient and productive lives. The role these mothers, other-mothers and grandmothers play is the role of what Carole Boyce Davies calls 'Mother-healers'. They not only nurture and provide emotional support to their daughters but even help them resolve ambiguities and aspirations of their sexuality. Though these daughters forge an identity which is separate from their mothers, they frequently acknowledge that a part of themselves is truly of their mothers.

Alice Walker expresses this dimension of the Black mother's consciousness of self and race in the essay 'In Search of Our Mother's Gardens'. She says that it was to her mother that she went in search of the secret of Black woman's inheritance. She discovers that the Black mother, sometimes unconsciously and sometimes as conscious artist or writer, hands on the creative spark, 'The legacy of Black Strength', that ensures the progress of the race. Numerous other Black writers along with Walker have paid tribute to the Black mother as a Madona bringing salvation to her Black children.

Feminine perspectives emphasize the inclusion of women's experience(s) and focus on care, or some of what traditionally have been considered feminine virtues, in particular, nurturance and compassion. Feminine perspectives typically celebrate virtues traditionally perceived as feminine and experiences that are peculiar to woman, such as pregnancy, labour, childbirth and nursing. In contrast, *feminist* perspectives take women to be in oppressed position *vis-à-vis* men, and they focus on that position and the structures that have contributed to women's oppression. A feminist perspective has three features: A recognition that women as a group have been and are oppressed, an account of the source or sources of that oppression; and suggestions for how the oppression of women can be overcome. A helpful guiding statement comes from Tong in *Feminine and Feminist Ethics*:

> "Clearly, feminist approaches to ethics have a different set of goals than feminine and maternal approaches to ethics. Whereas feminine and maternal approaches tend to focus more on retrieving women's 'feminine' values from the netherworld of patriarchal neglect, feminist approaches tend to focus on criticizing those values to determine where they add to or subtract from women's oppression. A feminist approach to ethics is always interested in issues of power—specifically male domination and female subordination, and it always seeks to provide women with action guides that will lead to women's liberation from oppression, suppression and repression." (Tong 184)[1]

For the Liberal feminist, the suppression of women into mothering and caring role is based not only in the public/private dichotomy but also in false claims about women's nature. They see mothering as socialized and oppressive gender roles rather than evidence of a feminine nature shared by all women. In the liberal feminist view, when all are afforded equal opportunities, all women may freely choose to 'mother' or not to 'mother'.

A second feminist approach to ethics comes from Marxist feminism. Marxist feminism theory itself finds nothing intrinsically degrading about childbearing, child rearing, caring, etc. But instead Marxist theory criticizes the way in which these tasks are organized under capitalism. In this sense, Marxist feminist theory could be said to be 'about' mothering and caring. Thus mothering would be described by a Marxist feminist as part of exploitation at home and asserts that the oppression will only be overcome when the domestic work that is done by women is transformed.

A third feminist approach to mothering is tied to the Radical feminist view. Mothering and caring, as they serve the patriarchal social order, are causes of women's oppression. Women's reproductive roles and responsibilities as well as institution of compulsory heterosexuality, are the fundamental causes of women's subordination and men's domination. Radical feminists affirm the importance of love between women, agreeing that the ideal of the feminist woman who knows herself and is not afraid to love herself and other women must replace the ideal of the feminine woman who lives only for her children and for men. In the specific sense the mothering is asserted to be casual factor of the subordination of women according to radicals. Radical feminists differ from Marxist feminists in that as Marxist feminists do not assert that mothering and caring as institutions should be eliminated, but that the overriding capitalist and classed system should be eliminated, one aspect of radical feminism's sufficient conditions for women's liberation is the elimination of institutions like the family.

A fourth feminist approach to this issue would be related to Socialist feminism. This branch recognizes that much of women's energy has been consumed in sexual and procreative labour as mothering and caring and most of this labour has always been forced rather than free. Women are alienated as mothers because they do not control the conditions of their motherhood. Jagger lists many social and technological issues women have faced as mothers, noting that 'the increasing subjection of the domestic childbearing process to scientific control suggests that mother's experience is parallel in this respect to the experience of wage labourers. The condition of modern women's oppression as seen by the socialist feminist view leads to the conclusion that women's liberation requires totally new models of organizing all forms of production and final abolition of femininity. Mothering, in a socialist feminist framework, is a central experience of many oppressed women, be it Indian or American. Women novelists hailing from totally different cultural contexts take up the interior journey of a human being as mother. Anita Desai, Shashi Deshpande, Shobha Dé, Toni Morrison, Alice Walker and Paule Marshall; all have voiced their feelings about the woman's role of mother in their novels. Maya Angelou avowed:

> "There is a kind of strength that is most frightening in Black women. It's as if a steel rod runs right through her head down to the feet. And I believe that we have to thank Back women not only for keeping the Black family alive, but (also) the white family .... Because Black woman have nurtured a nation of strangers. For hundreds of years, they literally nursed babies at their breasts who they know, when they grew up, would, rape their daughters and kill their sons."[2]

Black women seemed to embrace the myth of matriarchy. Nancy Chowdow's *The Reproduction of Mothering* (1978) is perhaps the most important and impressive feminist interpretation of Freudian theory. Her central thesis is that gender personality is shaped by black women who have written the psychodynamics of the family, in particular within the 'object-relations', the child forms, especially with the mother. Women seek other outlet for their emotional needs than men. It impels them, in short, toward motherhood where with their own children they can recreate the emotional bonding that they need. The woman's mental make-up is thus ideally suited for the role of motherhood.

> "As long as women mother, we can expect that a girl's preoedipal period will be longer than that of a boy and that women, more than man, will be more open to and preoccupied with those very rational issues that go into mothering—feelings of identification, lack of separateness or differentiation."[3]

In Toni Morrison's novels this echo of the mother's voice extracts her from the framework of stereotyped black motherhood. Highly individualized mothers are presented in the context of their history. Of the two parents the mother was more likely to be available to the children. An aspect of this matriarchalism that we see in the novels of Morrison is the bonding with the daughters. The sons either die, run away or appear just on the fringes of the story. When the sons do something terrible and have to be 'put outdoors' the mothers do it. The creative inheritance passes through the daughter and unlike the sons she will stay and fight the suffocating influence of the mother. In essence the mother is for the child, a source of arbitrary power and symbolizes the maternal genealogy, in the role of the executor of the patriarchal will.

It is not uncommon to have the image of the 'mother terrible' in Morrison's novels. Sethe was convinced that death could provide a better existence to Beloved than a slave-life could. In 'Tar Baby' Morrison takes on the role of the daughter. She defines herself Jadine in opposition to the maternal figure and is sympathetic to Jadine's plight and critical of the negative aspects of mothering. Matriarchal power, always ambiguous in Morrison's novels, includes the equally ambiguous power to name, and a primary example of this is Eva in Sula. The mothers, 'the ancestor figures', as Morrison often refers to them, are the primary names in Morrison's novels, just as they are the transmitters of culture and the inventors of language, itself the operative agency of culture. It is they who always 'say the important things'.

This relational self, which constitutes such an important pattern in Morrison's fictions, derives at least as much from the strong bonding among her female characters as it does from racial identification. The biological states of pregnancy and of motherhood itself, in Morrison's terms, are experienced as a splitting of the self. In 'Beloved', Sethe recounts her feelings to Beloved:

> "You asleep on my back. Denver sleep in my Stomach. Felt like I was split in two."[4]

No father, no man, can understand, according to Sethe, that this condition is less a splitting than a spreading, a dissolution of boundaries, an embrace of multiplicity. Of Paul D's reaction to the murder of her child, Sethe says,

> "Too thick, he said my love was too thick ...... When I fell you you mine, I also mean I'm yours. I wouldn't draw breath without my children."[5]

Perhaps the closest we can come in theoretical terms to understanding Morrison's rendering of motherhood is in Kristeva's argument in 'Women's Time'.

> "Pregnancy seems to be experienced as the radical ordeal of the splitting of the subject, redoubling up of the body, ... The arrival of the child, on the other hand, leads the mother into the labyrinths of an experience that, without the child, she would only rarely encounter love for an other."[6]

Cixous, too, sees motherhood as the ultimate subversion of male-defined subjectivity in 'The Laugh of the Medusa'. She writes:

> "The mother, too, is a metaphor. It is necessary and sufficient that the best of herself be given to woman by another woman for her to be able to love herself and return in love the body that was 'born' to her. Touch one, caress me, you the living no name, give me myself as myself."[7]

In Morrison's mother-daughter relationships, no Lacanian mirror interferes with the preoedipal relationship, that are sometimes destructive yet also potentially positive arrangement which occurs in each one of Morrison's novels. Also like nature, the ultimate power of which is greater than that of history, the Black mother can kill as well as create, she is Kali as well as Demeter, and the image of the 'Phallic mother' is always problematic for Morrison.

The concept of mothering is equally important for Indian women novelists writing in English. Anita Desai, Shashi Deshpande and Shobha Dé represents this thought in their work of art. In *Voices in the City*, Nirode wants to systematically reject his past, his upbringing, his family wealth and tradition—above all he wants to reject his mother. The traditional Indian concept of motherhood easily translates into a willing tolerance of a life of sacrifice, suffering and exploitation. The mother, especially if she happens to be a widow, is expected to possess archetypal fortitude and follow an intensively rigid moral patterns of life. Nirode's ambivalent attitude towards his mother is a product of this unconscious social conditioning. He is mesmerized by his mother's grace and refinement, but wants to relate to her only in a traditional manner. His mother's aloof independence and continued friendship with Major Chadha repulses him and almost in a revengeful mood he spurns her help and prefers and his incapacity to empathize with her gradually and viciously grips her conscience. Nirode's anger at his mother's capacity to retain her individuality and consciousness of his own inability to accept it are crudely palpable in his advice to Amla to learn from her mother's experiences of love. Nirode's ultimate acceptance of his mother's individuality finally enables him to understand his own life in a more balanced and rational manner. It is the male sexuality that defines all that a woman is where sexuality exists for someone else who is socially male. Women have been part of mothering theory values, women have learnt as part of the cultural practices attached to motherhood, enlarging it to the notion of motherland counting.

Nirode's psychic imbalance has stemmed from his unresolved love-hate relationship with his mother. Once he is able to overcome his blinkered mindset, negate his prejudices about motherhood and perceive the independent status of his mother as a person, he is able to turn back to his life in a positive mood. We find that with the accidental death of the father, there is a tendency in all the siblings, Nirode, Amla and Monisha to crave for the love of the mother. But in her sophistication and in her capacity, to have men around her to flatter her, she is not motherly enough to her children. She is too airy to understand her children.

Shashi Deshpande has presented the conflict between mother and daughter in her novels. There are also good mothers and daughters, like there is Vanar and her mother in *The Binding Vine*. But Saru and her mother has a very bad conflict. Jaya has problems with her mother, that doesn't mean she doesn't love her mother. And conflict between Saru and her mother is also a plausible and credible thing because such things do happen. People expect the love between mother and daughter to be very iovy and dovy, totally self-less mothers and daughters. But it is not so in real life.

Shobha Dé deliberately ignores the sanctity of motherhood as prescribed by man in her novels. In *Starry Nights* she presents a different kind of mother-daughter relationship. Aasha Rani before becoming a film star was Viji, bastard child of a film-producer. After the father deserts Viji's family, in order to survive, her mother pushes her into the underworld of blue films. Scared Viji breakes into tears but has to submit to her mother's command. In order to earn money, her mother takes her to Bombay and as she has a voluptuous figure, with the help of a small-time producer Kisten Bhal, she is able to get a film contract. Her mother, acting as her first-pimp, compels her to 'please' big personalities of cinema in order to get good roles. But later on she plans for her daughter Sasha something different. She wants to give her daughter what she could not receive from her mother.

Finally we can conclude in the words of Marianna Hersch. In her essay 'Maternal Narratives: Cruel Enough to Stop the Blood', she illustrates the relationship between feminism and the maternal instinct. I feel 'woman' and 'mothering' are two inseparable elements. But as radical feminists say 'mothering' or 'no mothering' should be a personal choice of a particular woman: Mother can be good or bad, selfish or selfless but mother plays an important part in the life of her child.

REFERENCES

1. Tong, "Femine and Feminist Ethics," www.yahoo.com.
2. Maya Angelou, quoted in Jel 45 (Dec 23, 1973), 48.
3. "Psychology Constructs the Female," in Gomick and Moran *Woman in Sexist Society* Garden City Dowdedane, 1972, 133-146.
4. Toni Morrison, *Beloved,* 202.
3. *Ibid.*, 203.
6. Julia Kristeva; "Women's Time," 1981, 26, Signs 7, 1.
7. Hélèn Cixous, "The Laugh of the Medusa," Manchester: Manchester University Press, 313.

16 Violence Against Women

While not all men are violent; men in general tend to be more violent, than women. Biologists cite the male hormone testosterone as a kickstarter for aggressive behaviour in men. While the hormone affects male attitudes and the propensity toward violence, they stress that as humans, we make individual choices whether to be aggressive or not.

Violence against women has been accepted and even condoned throughout history. More than 2,000 years ago, Roman law gave a man life and death authority over his wife. In the 18th century, English common law gave a man permission to discipline his wife and children with a stick or whip no wider than his thumb. This 'rule of thumb' prevailed in England and America until the late 19th century. Many feminists claim that violence against women is the result of a deeply enhanced patriarchal culture that encourages and rewards male domination. They say that in a patriarchal culture, men are more likely to use violence to keep their dominant position. While society claims to abhor violence, we often make heroes of men who are aggressive. In the culture of masculinity, heroes are often predicated on some kind of violent action. The traditional model of masculinity encourages men to exude an aura of daring and aggression. For most Americans, including many feminists, the violence issues were disturbing. They revealed women at their most vulnerable and men at their worst. Violence against women as an area of study for feminists is a recent one. Feminists have not studied this area specifically and in an agreed upon manner until the recent past. However, since the early 80s violence against women has became extremely important for feminists and this project hopes to understand and makes contribution to the present feminist debates regarding the object of study.

All too commonly, whether implicitly or explicitly, women are the 'other'. Consequently, it becomes necessary in the eyes of those who seek power over to control and belittle women, and all aspects of womanhood. In many cultures women are viewed as the possessions of their men. Therefore, when a woman is raped, it is effectively an attack on the manhood of her man. Using this reasoning, women become the targets of war in order to attack the honour of the men of a particular culture, ethnic group or country. For these reasons, rape and other forms of sexual assault against women are always a part of war and conflict. The time has come when we can no longer deny that misogynist violence is a major component of militaristic power over thinking, as well as a significant part of the global pandemic of violence against women. But we must go beyond that and recognize the reality that 'men's violence against women' is so prevalent, that even in 'peacetime', there is no peace for women.

A vital part of understanding a social problem and a precursor to preventing it, must concentrate on factors of what causes it. Research on causes of violence against women has consisted of two lines of enquiries. First, examination of the characteristics that influence the behaviour of offenders; second, consideration of whether some women have a lightered vulnerability to victimisation. Research has sought causal factors at various levels of analysis, including individual, institutional and social characteristics of offending, and victimisation remain conceptually distinct. It can be seen through naked eyes that whenever and wherever there is exploitation, oppression and violence, woman is the worst sufferer.

According to *Webster's International Dictionary*, violence is a force, which injures or abuses. Such a meaning of 'violence' includes both personal injury and property damage. *The Thesaurus* indicates that the noun 'violence' connotes vehemence, impetuosity, vigorousness, excess, destructiveness, vandalism, turbulence, turmoil, roughness, severity, brute-force, brutality, savagers, mercilessness, exacerbation and explosion. The adjective 'violent' is explained among other terms by the terms aggressive, charging, disorderly, turbulent, stormy, anarchistic, nihilistic, intemperate and immoderate.

According to SNDT University's Research Centre for Women's Studies, "Violence, in general, is a coercive mechanism to assent one's will over another, in order to prove or feel a sense of a power. Those in power against the powerless can perpetuate it. Any individual or group facing the threat of coercion or being disciplined to act in a manner required by another individual or group is subject to violence."[1]

To combat violence one must first understand it. The breakthrough has come with the feminist movement which has been able to conceptualise violence in terms of an inevitable manifestation of the patriarchal system, a system resting on and vesting in the subordination and exploitation of a woman, a system that is age-old and worldwide. 'Violence Against Women' the term makes the sense of pain that is more painful than any other pain which includes the sense of fear also. In behavioural terms, violence against women ranges from simple suppression to abuse, aggression, exploitation and severe oppression. It also includes rape, wife-beating, and denial of education to girls, harassment physically as well as mentally. Thus all such kinds make the term more terrible.

Various researches on violence against women suggest that violence arises from interactions among individual biological and psychological factors and social processes. Violent behaviour is not caused by any single factor, much of time research has focused on single cause factor. Some explanations focused on mental disorder or personality traits and profiles; some on social learning models that shape individual men to be violent. It includes social information processing theory concerning the cognitive process that offenders engage in before, during and after violence. Socio-cultural analyses aimed at understanding the structural features of society at the level of family, peer group, religion and state that encourage male violence and maintain women as a vulnerable class of potential victims. Moreover, it gives feminist explanations stressing the gendered nature of violence against women and its roots in patriarchal social system.

It is theorised that males who have difficulty in obtaining partners are mere likely to resort to sexual coercion or rape. Evolutionary theory also has been theorised that male sexual jealousy developed as a means of assuring the paternity of their offsprings. Case histories from battered women often mention the extreme sexual jealousy displayed by their batterers and extreme sexual jealousy is a common motive of men who kill their wives.

However, evolutionary explanations and feminist theorist acknowledge that additional factors are necessary to explain sexual assault and intimate partner violence. Among the rest of causes, ALCOHOL is one of them. Every category of aggressive act has higher prevalence among people who have been drinking. Researches link drinking and alcohol abuse to physical aggression. The relationship of alcohol to intimate partner violence could be specious. The drinking habit spoils the relationship of husband and wife. It takes off the sense of responsibility from the male side.

Alcoholism increases violence against women by torturing them both physically and mentally. Famous Afro-American novelist and poetess Alice Walker has written; that is apt to describe the alcoholism as a cause of violence against women. I quote:

> I drink to our ruined house,
> to the dolor of my life,
> to our loneliness together
> and to you. I rouse my glass,
> to lying lips that have betrayed us,
> to dead-cold, pitiless eyes,
> and to the hard realities;
> that the world is brutal and coarse,
> that cold in fact has not saved us.[2]

The relationship of alcohol to violence is a complex one involving physiological, psychological, and socio-cultural factors. Alcohol has been associated with effects on aggression. Studies have found a genetic basis for alcohol abuse and alcoholism, and for anti-social personality traits that can be found among violent offenders.

Psychopathology and personality traits played a great role in violence against women. A number of studies have found a high incidence of psychopathology and personality disorder among men who assault their wives. Attitudes and gender scripts are another cause of violence against women. Cultural myths about violence, gender scripts and roles, sexual scripts and roles, and male entitlements are represented at the individual level as attitudes and similarly culturally sanctioned beliefs about the rights and privileges of husbands have historically legitimised a man's domination over his wife and warranted his use of violence to control her. Men in general are more accepting of men abusing women, and the most culturally traditional men are the most accepting. Batterers often excuse their wives' unwifely behaviour as their justification.

Sex and power motives are other determinants of violence against women. The view conjures the image of a powerful man, who uses violence against women as a tool to maintain his superiority. Power and control frequently underline intimate partner violence, but the purpose of the violence may also be in response to man's feeling of powerlessness and inability to accept rejection. Society is another causal factor in the determination of violence against women. Since the ancient time society never gave justified status to woman, violence naturally springs from unsolved social problems. Many feminist writers have suggested that pornography encourages the objectification of women, endorses and condones sexual aggression towards women. Pornography has been found to increase men's aggression towards women. It appears that the depiction of violence against women is more than sexual explicitness and attitudes that are accepting such violence. The feminist analysis of violence against women is at heart, a critic of patriarchy. The central argument is that the brutalisation of an individual wife by an individual husband is not an individual or family problem. It is simply one manifestation of the system of male domination of female that has existed historically and crossed-culturally. Societal tolerance of wife beating is a reflection of patriarchal norms that more generally support male dominance in marriage. Traditional marriage in turn is a central element of patriarchal society. Del Martin, a noted feminist analyst of wife beating, writes in *Battered Wives*.

> "The historical roots of our patriarchal family models are ancient and deep... New norms for marriage and family must be created, since the battering of wives grows naturally out of ancient and time-honored traditions."[3]

Martin provides an overview of the cruelty directed at women, and wives in particular—throughout history for centuries, husbands have tortured and killed disobedient wives with the support of the state and the church. Physical violence against women in the name of chastisement was legal in the United States. Martin concludes, "Marriage is the mechanism by which the patriarchy is maintained."[4]

A more scholarly volume on violence against women that follows the lines of Martin's work is Dobash's *Violence Against Wives*.

They assert that:

> "... man who assault their wives are actually living up to cultural prescriptions that are cherished in western society—aggressiveness, male dominance, and female subordination—and they are using physical force as a means to enforce that dominance."[5]

Historical causes of violence against women are incomplete without discussing the religion, which is the backbone of the patriarchal society. Christianity and other patriarchal religions affirmed the male dominating family structure. The husband was held responsible for his wife's behaviour and was admonished to beat her when she committed a serious wrong or mortal sin. The beatings then were for the protection of the woman's soul.

Law has its own role in determining the violence against women. William Blackstone confirmed, "By marriage the husband and wife are one person in law, that is the very being or legal existence of the women is suspended in marriage."[6]

Family court, where reconciliation is the primary concern, serves the husbands' interest by decriminalising his behaviour, coercing a victim into reconciling and living with her batterer is not only an injustice but highly dangerous. Violence if unchecked, escalates and increases in frequency and severity. It is generally accepted that multiple classes of influence, from the individual to the macro level, determine the expression of assault and sexually aggressive behaviour in man that causes violence against woman. "The goal of feminism," according of Faye Powell, "became to eliminate, sexist oppresson, imposed by patriarchal society and discriminations against women on the job, in the home and in all areas of women's lives."[7]

Weakening family and community ties in the modern era have not been replaced with alternative modes of human commitment and social organization. The denial of human emotional needs such as bonding, trust, affection and a shared spiritual orientation to life in the modern world has resulted in a plethora of pathological behaviours ranging from greed, dominance, wife-beating, child-abuse, drug-abuse, callousness and violence to obsessive needs. In patriarchal culture, power is equated with aggression and masculinity; weakness with compassion and femininity. Women are supposed to bear male oppression silently and meekly. Where they fail to do so, they are branded as 'loud', hysterical, crazy and frequently punished with rape and physical assault.

As feminist analysts suggest, male desire to dominate and conquer may result from a deep psychological insecurity stemming from men's inability to give birth to life. The feminist movements of the sixties and after, served as guiding force to female writers and they took up the challenge of establishing their separate canon in literature. They discovered that not only the flesh and blood women but also even the women caged in words and pages of a text were constrained into the bonds of patriarchal culture. These female writers tried to understand how social imposition and restriction shaped women's lives with and without the pages of book. Having seen the varied ways in which women had been oppressed, trivialised and misrepresented by the particular writers, these scholars sought to change the status of women in society as well as in literature. Virginia Woolf's *A Room of One's Own*, Simone de Beauvior's *The Second Sex* and Kate Millett's *Sexual Politics* are the few instances of this awareness.

Feminists and sociologists have come to certain terms and suggested some measures to prevent the atrocities on women. This starts with socially redefining of 'violence against women'. Women have to say things publicly which they dared not say before. Strengthening up the women organisation is also recommended. If a group of women of like minded views join together, form an organisation and raise their voice against the sufferings of women, they can make an impact. These feminist and social organisations should create an awareness among women to struggle against their oppression and to fight the persons who exploit, humiliate and torture the women. They may hold protest marches, demonstrations and public meetings in different areas and localities, provide emotional support to women victims, pressurize the police to act speedily, organize orientation camps for women for educating them about their rights and laws relating to these.

It is also necessary to develop a humanistic approach to the victims of violence against women. There should be changes in attitudes and values of judicial officials, the establishment of family courts, and a change in police attitude. The circumstantial evidence should be given importance in the court of law.

The crimes against women deserve a scientific and psychological study and the victims of crimes require an objective approach in our reactions and a more humanistic response in the dealings.

Finally, we can sum up this discussion with a point that when a women suffers from physical and sexual abuse, this leads her to suffer psychologically too. Consequently it affects the family and especially children. Because family is a small unit of society, it naturally affects the social environment. Thus to check the chain of disadvantages of violence against women feminists law makers, sociologists and literary artists all turn such negative forces into the construction of something positive. Just as to move the boat, boatman uses his force into opposite direction; similarly feminists used this negative term violence to enforce the new spirit in the women. The main outcome of all these violence against women ultimately will lead women to raise their voices and fight against violence. Like Walker's *Meridian* they will proclaim:

> "There is water in the world for us
> brought by our friends
> though the rock of mother and god
> vanishes into sand
> and we, cast out alone
> to heal
> and re-create
> ourselves."[8]

REFERENCES

1. Yashode Bhatt, *The Image of Woman in Indian Literature*, New Delhi: B.R. Publishing Corporation, 1993, 67.
2. Alice Walker, *Meridian*, N.Y., Washington: Square Press, 1976, 127.
3. D. Martin, Battered Wives, San Francisco: Vocano Press, 1981, 26.
4. *Ibid.*, 37.
5. R.E. Dobash and R. Dobash, *Violence Against Wives: A Case Against the Patriarchy*, New York: Free Press, 1979, 24.
6. W. Blackstone, "Commentaries on the Law of England", New York: Oceand, 1966, 442.
7. Faye Powell, "African-American Feminist Issues: An Overview" *IJAS,* 20.1, Winter 1990, 2.
8. Alice Walker, *Meridian*, N.Y., Washington: Square Press, 1976, 212.

17 Doctrine of Separate Spheres: A Feminist Concern or a Myth

The doctrine of Separate Spheres for men and women is the part of various societies and social norms. It is deemed that men are less emotional, more rational, as well as physically better able to stand the stern and ruthless world of the marketplace. However, women need the protecting walls of home because they are weak. They also have other qualities, derived in large part from their maternal nature that make them specially fitted to be both protectors as well as protected. These were the softer virtues of patience, gentleness and loving kindness, which they can use to succor and comfort their husbands and their children.

This doctrine of separate spheres was challenged by the feminists who claimed for women the right to break out of both their confinement to domesticity and their legal and political subordination to men. They had to re-examine for themselves both the cult of domesticity and its corollary, the doctrine of true womanhood, because these were not only the justification for woman's separate sphere but the basis on which the anti-feminists attacked the feminist's cause. In this process the feminists changed, sometimes in highly significant ways, the view of women's character and destiny without ever totally rejecting the basis of the doctrine, which implied not only a special feminine nature but also a grounding of that nature in women's domestic and ultimately her maternal role.

The opposition to the feminist demands was varied in its nature and sometimes rested on no more than a religious prescription that derived ultimately from the Adam and Eve myth. More frequent, however, was the argument that women's emancipation would unfit them for their domestic role, and particularly for their functions as mothers. In the eyes of some anti-feminists this argument was based quite simply on the belief that to admit women to exciting and perhaps lucrative creative employment or to involve women actively in the political process would make them discontented with the obscurity and even the tedium of their home bound lives. At a deeper level was the fear that experience of the world was dangerous for women; that their special characteristics of tenderness, affection and moral purity were a consequence not so much of innate differences between men and women as of the protection from the wickedness of the world that allowed the maintenance of that state of innocence on which women's nature depended.

To some extent the corrupting influence of experience of the world, and particularly of evil, was something that applied to both sexes. Frequently, however, the view was expressed that women were weaker than men, not only physically but also mentally and morally, so that their protection from evil was absolutely essential; if they were to remain pure and good. Thus, their lack of reasoning power, their lack of self-control, their failure to calculate consequences, were all put forward to explain women's special need for dependence. The claim that women were weaker than men was a powerful argument in opposition to the employment of women, especially, in areas that were regarded as male preserves.

In examining the feminist defence against these accusations, we have to consider the different traditions within feminism itself, for, although, there might be temporary alliances in support of particular goals, there was considerable variation in approach depending on whether the dominant tradition was primarily religious or reflected the more radical philosophy of the 'Enlightenment'.

Many feminists laid the emphasis that women had a special reforming role in society. She provided the rationale for the entry of large numbers of women into moral reform, whether in the cause of purity or temperance, which eventually led feminism into the attempt to use the vote to transform society itself. The cost however was that feminism was trapped into a view of womanhood that came dangerously close to the traditional view from which the feminists were trying to escape.

This is not to suggest, of course, that the feminist accepted the traditional view of women as they found it. In the hands even of the most conservative of them, the cult of domesticity become transformed into the ideal of female superiority and the doctrine of separate spheres into the attempted invasion of the masculine world not simply by women but, potentially even more revolutionary in its impact, by womanly values. Men called female as 'superior' and according to this new ideology, it was now the male who was naturally evil, the female was essentially good, and through her goodness and purity, she was able to redeem mankind from sin. Like the feminists, Ruskin also believed that women's mission was to rescue 'Humanity' from sin.

By the second half of the nineteenth century this ideal of female superiority appears to have gained wide acceptance not only amongst moral reformers (both male and female) but amongst women writers catering to the emotional needs of middle-class women not necessarily either feminists or moral reformers. The fiction of the period portrayed women not only as fundamentally different from men, but as basically superior creatures. Perhaps, however, the ideal of woman as moral saviour reached its fullest development at the close of the nineteenth century and in the early years of the twentieth century, which saw, particularly in the United States, the involvement of middle-class women in social reform on an unprecedented scale. The feminists in both Britain and the United States and later in India too, who fought against a separate curriculum in higher education, were certainly more concerned with women's economic independence than with their role as moral reformers and were anxious, indeed, to demonstrate in women those qualities of rationality that the anti-feminists deemed appropriate for men. They pursued the goal of opening to women the knowledge, skills and prestige previously reserved for men.

Apart from economic independence and political rights, feminists tended to base their arguments on women's moral superiority. Moreover, significantly, and even ironically, this concept of female superiority was carried over into the cult of celibacy, which became an important aspect of feminism by the end of the last century. Celibacy was important to the feminists because it attempted to set up an attentive role for women apart from the traditional female sphere of marriage and motherhood, an alternative, indeed, that was followed by man of the pioneers. It enabled them to avoid the sexual and economic subordination of marriage, while at the same time pursuing for themselves an internship and challenging career. This was true as many of the feminists chose to turn down offers of marriage in order to remain independent. And those who choose to marry were sometimes criticized for betraying the feminists cause. The urge for independence, however, far from arising from a desire to emulate men, may in some women have arisen from an aversion to masculine society.

Nevertheless, what is also clear is that even the rejection of marriage and maternity implicit in the choice of celibacy did not necessarily mean the rejection of the 'Feminine Mystique'. Olive Banks says, "The social worker and settlement workers in the closing years of the nineteenth century in both Britain and the United States were typical of the first generation of college women, many of whom chose to remain celibate in order to follow a career but who still saw that career in traditional role. They formed the basis of the 'social feminists' who O' Neill suggests took over from the radical feminists and gave nineteenth century feminism in particular its conservative character. Writing in the context of American feminism, O' Neill has criticized social feminism harshly for its failure to perceive the danger presented by even partial accommodation to the maternal mystique."[1]

If we conclude with Delamont and Duffin, that the feminists could not have pursued a more radical strategy, given all the circumstances in which they found themselves, it is still true that their acceptance of the maternal mystique was proved of a dangerous enterprise and one that ultimately led them 'back to the home from which feminism was supposed to liberate them'.

By the end of the nineteenth century feminism in both the United States and in Britain was, therefore, involved in contradictions between different definitions of feminism and different (and indeed) opposing concepts of femininity. Thus we have an opposition between women's rights and women's duty, between the similarities between men and women, between women's need for independence and their need for protection. These contradictions were not just between feminists and anti-feminists, as of course they were, but within feminism itself, and suggest indeed that there is not one feminism, but two. Moreover, these different aspects of feminism are all too often facing not only in different but actually in opposite directions, so that feminism is in a very real sense facing both ways.

By no means all the feminists were prepared to go alongwith Eleanor Rathbone in her views on the 'new feminisms', and Millicent Garrett Fawcett was strongly opposed to family endowment as weakening family responsibilities. The feminists like Eleaner Rathbone who wanted a new feminism based not upon equality but on women's special needs were still working within a traditional framework of women's roles.

New ideas on sexual morality were to transform the lives of women, especially to those of the middle class. Feminism as such was not in fact very important in producing these changes, but it clearly had to come to terms with them. Consequently, the twentieth century saw feminists exploring new attitudes on love and morality, marriage and divorce, contraception and abortion, and, perhaps most important of all, the nature and extent of female sexuality. The idea that sex was acceptable only for procreation steadily declined and there was a growing emphasis on the need for mutual sexual satisfaction. There was also a growing appreciation of the sexual needs of women, but female sexuality was still represented as more general, less diffuse and perhaps most significantly, less urgent than that of the male. The older generation of feminists, however, did not look approvingly at the growing sexual permissiveness. Many feminists like Gordan saw female sexuality as a trap to keep women pregnant and domesticated; but, instead of anticipating a time when women would be free to enjoy their sexuality, she looked forward to a society where there would be much less emphasis on sex.

An important part of the feminist's case was the need to free girls from a forced marriage. Economic independence, through educational and employment opportunities and changes in the law of property, was, in effect, the passport that enabled a woman not only to choose not to marry at all but even, under certain circumstances, to leave her husband. The feminists were therefore by no means traditional in their attitude to marriage and divorce. Nor did they expect women to submit in a docile way to the view of marriage that denied them rights to a legal identity and placed them in peripheral subordination to their husbands. Right into the twentieth century, the organized feminists were respectable, even puritan, in their attitude to marriage. In so far as they wished to equalize the legal position of women and men in divorce, it was simply to free wives from dissolute husbands and not in any sense to win more sexual freedom for themselves. The concept of 'free love' was therefore used by these feminists as a personal and individual response to the social and legal constraints that a conventional marriage laid upon them. By remaining free, they hoped to retain not only their independence but those rights that in spite of some changes in the law, they had lost on marriage including rights over the custody of their children. Indeed, easier and cheaper divorce was seen by some feminists as against the interests of women. This was largely due to the belief that easier divorce would allow men, in particular, to treat marriage more lightly. The issue of divorce has always reflected some of the ambiguities that the feminists have felt about marriage, seeing it sometimes as heaven, sometimes as trap. It is not surprising, therefore, if divorce has been seen by the feminists as largely an issue of equal rights, whether in the custody of children or the transfer of property. It is only with the modern movement that some of the deeper questions raised not only by divorce but by marriage itself have become central issues of feminism as a whole.

Consequently, we find a group of feminists, often known to one another, who not only combined their feminism with socialism but advocated, for women as well as for men, freedom to indulge in sexual pleasure as well as the economic independence sought by the more orthodox feminists. Often involved for a time at least, in 'free unions', they also advocated crèches and other types of communal facilities for working women as well as a motherhood endowment fund.

Radical feminism has also shown a deep concern with the issue of female sexuality. To some extent this concern has never been absent from the feminist movement, from its earliest days it has criticized the way in which women have been made the victims of male lust, both within and outside marriage. The attempt to redefine sexuality is combined with a new look at the effect of sexual permissiveness on women. Increasingly, greater sexual freedom has come to be seen as a doubtful benefit, operating as it does in the interests of men rather than women. Much feminist thinking has therefore gone into the problem of how to allow women sexual freedom without contributing to their domination, and it is in this control that we must understand the preoccupation with such issues as abortion law reform and, on a wider front, the attack on male-dominated medicine and the demand, central not only to radical feminism, but to feminists of almost every kind, that in political decisions and in personal relationships women are allowed to control their own bodies.

For some radical feminists the elimination of male domination would free the world not only of the oppression of the female by the male but of oppression itself. The pro-woman version of feminism accepts that sexism involves sex-role stereotyping but argues that procreation and children have been made to be oppressive by men. The removal of male domination would allow women not only to be free but also to be female. While some radical feminists like Firestone want to free women from biological maternity, there is another version of feminism that seeks only to free maternity from male domination. This involves on the one hand the return of childbirth to the care of women themselves and on the other the progressive removal of the rights and duties of fatherhood. The goal of such a version of feminism is neither equal rights nor androgyny, but matriarchy.

It has been one of the weaknesses of feminism that women as a whole have not been enthusiastic feminists. There have always been prominent women to argue an anti-feminist cause, and this is as true today as it was in the nineteenth century. Women, too, are always prominent in anti-feminist organizations. For much of its history feminism has appealed to a small minority of women and it is only occasionally, more recently, at the start of the new feminism, that it begins to approach a mass movement. However, even on such a feminist issue as abortion, women as a whole are less likely to support it than are men.

Women's organizations, on the other hand, while not necessarily feminists, have at times rallied to support feminist goals, and one important aspect of most successful feminist campaigns has been the way in which the support of women's groups, that are not normally overtly feminist, provides not merely numbers but the appearance. What then can be said about the future of feminism? Clearly it would be foolish to assume that the present level of feminist activity will continue, and there are in fact already signs that perhaps it has passed its peak. Nor is it safe to assume that the setback to women's aspirations in the field of employment will lead to a heightening of feminist consciousness. The rise of the one-parent family has already been mentioned, since it provides both men and women with experiences that take them outside the traditional division of labour within the family. There is also some evidence that fathers spend more time with their children, even if only in the more 'attractive' aspect of child care. Given that this trend continues, it may go some way to break down the rigid sex-role stereotyping that, by seeing women as 'natural' mothers, denies fathers both the physical care of young children and the qualities of caring and tenderness that are associated with this role. Moreover, recent moves, often feminist inspired to reduce sex typing in schools and to break down the stereotyping of men's and women's occupations will, if they succeed, challenge the traditional division of labour in the workplace.

Such developments suggest that notions of femininity and masculinity may be less rigid in the future as women are allowed to develop more of their 'male' and men more of their 'female' nature. Role sharing within marriage is possible, but it cuts cross the demands of the work situation, threatening a highly competitive career and depriving the husband of much of his leisure time. For a few families, paid domestic help is at least a partial solution, for others the decision not to have children, but for most couples the answer lies in structural changes that allow a greater community involvement in child care or, alternatively in a change in the nature of work that enables it to combine with domestic responsibilities rather than to conflict with them. This would allow both husbands and wives to participate on equal terms in the world of work and in the care of children within the family. The goal of androgyny, therefore, does not depend simply on changing attitudes, although this is necessarily a part of it. All of this, however, implies some level of agreement about the nature of feminism. Feminists themselves differ in their assessment both of what is wrong with the position of women in society and of what is needed to put it right.

Various labels ranging from 'Female consciousness' to 'Difference feminism', transform social policy in the name of family protection and decide separate spheres for men and women. Maternalism is a double-edged sword. Women might be mobilized as mothers to gain rights, but they could also be confined as mothers to a dependent economic and political role. Opponents of suffrage invoked materialism when they insisted that women exercised more authority as mothers than they would as voters. By setting up an opposition between motherhood and citizenship, anti-suffragists retained both the ideology of separate spheres and the principle of covertures, in which a husband represented the economic and political interests of his wife. Feminists had to walk a thin line, balancing their identities as mothers with their demands for equality. Also like later radical feminisms, it rested upon essentialists' notions of a common womanhood that ignored class differences and presumed female were superior. Finally, it is clear, that the seemingly paradoxical beliefs in gender equality and gender difference would continue to characterize modern feminism. Gilman's gender analysis attempted to transcend the limitations of separate spheres ideology and resolve the paradox of difference. "In addition to 'sharply defined and quite different' spheres for woman and man, she added that 'there remains a common sphere—that of humanity, which belongs to both alike."[2]

The common sphere, however, often resembled a female rather than male model.

REFERENCES

1. Olive Banks, *Faces of Feminism*, New York: St. Mastin's Press, 1981, 98.
2. Quoted in Corinne A. Perner, "Chilean Feminists: The International Women's Movement and Suffrage, 1915-1950" *Pacific Historical Review*, 69: 4 (2000), 668-69.

18

Femininity Vs Masculinity

"Patriarchal ideology", according to Kate Millet, "exaggerates biological differences between men and women, making certain that men always have the dominant, or 'masculine', roles and that women always have the subordinate, or 'feminine ones'."[1] In this context, one central problem derives from the need to give consent to the concepts of masculinity and femininity, something that is usually achieved by reference to the attachment/separation problematic, developed by feminist psychologists.

The female subject is the eternally feminine 'source of life, power and energy'. Feminist reader looks towards politics of gender. French version of 'feminine' refers to femaleness or femininity. Sex and gender are theoretical constructs. Sex is a biological category, whereas gender is a socio-cultural category. Female body is represented in culture. To show feminine, from Plato to Freud has been perceived in terms of matter, physics, passion, emotions, and the irrational characteristics traditionally associated with nature. Patriarchal values are consciously imported into language. Masculinity and masculism into man, result a kind of essentialist which refers to the 'unconscious determinants of patriarchal cultures' than the conscious reasoning behind them. The term 'femininity' refers to social and cultural construction of women, wherein they are shaped differently not only in terms of representation of body but also in relation to institutionalised role performances, internalisation of values and conformity to cultural practices. There are some aspects of the biological make-up of women, which are of the greatest potentialities for producing distinctive female behaviour. The greatest simple structural difference of woman occurs at the moment of conception when, as a single cell, she starts out possessing two X chromosomes instead of the male's single X chromosome. This single difference is the prime cause of all the later differentiated differences. Upto about the age of seven, both male and female are essentially the same in their endocrinologic and physiologic functioning. Then begins a divergence of sex endocrine functions. The girl begins to produce definitely more estrogen than does the boy, and this difference steadily increases to puberty by the age of about ten, this increased estrogen function in the girl is sufficient to produce discernible sex characters. Then comes the tremendous change of full puberty and the onset of menstrual periods at menarche. No matter how the girl has been mentally and emotionally prepared for this; there is no denying of the tremendous behavioural impact of the biological event itself. There are certain obvious conclusions about its influence on women's behaviour. First of all, the very fact that the woman has approximately a monthly cycle of tremendous hormonal variation constitutes a marked difference from the physiology of the man. Males have no such regular rhythm in hormonal variation or indeed any comparable hormonal changes. In the premenstrum there is a tendency to depression, irritability, emotional instability, hair trigger emotional response, decreased concentration ability, increased frequency of headaches and other personality changes. Whatever minor neurotic traits a woman may possess, these traits tend to be exaggerated by her premenstrual physiology. The implications with regard to the behaviour of women are, of course, enormous. For example, the highest suicide rate among women occurs in premenstrual week. The effect on marital and family relations is obvious and sometimes far reaching to put it mildly.

This brings us then to the most significant difference between men and women, that is woman's role in human reproduction. She can bear a child while a man cannot. Moreover, man's role in the reproductive process is a very short, transient one while woman's starts from that episode and stretches out through nine months of gestation. During this time she is subject to all sorts of very extensive changes in body symptoms and functions. Besides various physiological changes, she becomes increasingly vulnerable to the daily threats of modern life. She becomes increasingly dependent on the labours of others for her own survival. Finally, she has the extraordinary experience, trauma, joy and threat of the birth processes to go through. It seems almost unnecessary to say that the behavioural implications to woman of the gestational and birth processes, are so extraordinarily extensive that they will doubtless be the subject of speculation and study as long as mankind exists. Psychiatrists and psychologists would agree that they have scarcely scratched the surface of woman's psychological reactions to her reproductive function. Certainly this is the major and most overwhelming aspect of woman's biological nature as it affects what she does, what she thinks, and how her emotions impel her.

But after woman's reproductive life is over, she presents another important biological feature uniquely female, that is, the climacteric, the menopause. At this time, due to certain endocrinologic changes, there are extensive bodily changes. The man has no such sudden climacteric. As the feminist influences of extrogen is withdrawn, the woman experiences many physiological changes. Alongwith these come variable degrees of emotional instability, irritability, depression, lack of concentration, weepiness, headaches, and the like. And especially striking at this time may be an aggravation of the neurotic component of a woman's personality.

Apart from the biological differences, there are well-established sex differences in several mental and intellectual abilities. It has been an interesting area of study for the psychologists and they have through a series of experiments arrived at the conclusion that:

> "The masculinity-femininity contrast is probably as deeply grounded, whether by nature or nurture, as any other, which human temperament presents."[2]

They have established on the basis of attitude interest analysis of masculinity-femininity test that males posses more self-assertion and aggressiveness, greater hardships and boldness and more roughness of manner, expressions and sentiments. The females on the other hand, have different and contrary personality traits. They are in general more kind and compassionate, more timid, more fastidious and aesthetically sensitive and more emotional. At the same time females exhibit a greater degree of awareness, achievement drive and emotional drive. Similar is the opinion of the behavioural psychologists like Rosenkrantz, Vogel, Bee and Broverman about women. According to them they are gentle and are in strong need for security. They are tender in feeling and sensitive to art and literature, whereas men are aggressive, independent, active and unemotional. Various points are raised by R.S. Tiwari in his essay, "Feminism and Globalization versus Indian Women Empowerment". I quote:

> "Men's power in society is of high degree and they defined morality and culture.
>
> — Men form the customs, laws and opinions for women. Lesbianism is the expression of womanhood.
>
> — Economic freedom, resource redistribution and political representation are essential for empowerment.
>
> — Domestic labour is a burden and men have used the sex based division of labour to restrict the role of women and their development.
>
> — Personal autonomy is important and women are forced to sacrifice many things in the name of family, society, wider public interests, etc., which is unjust.
>
> — Purity and uncorrupted values are imposed upon women by men and their society.
>
> — Western movement with their culture is appreciable since it provides more freedom to women.
>
> — The problem of treating women-work as unproductive.
>
> — The situation of dependence that women suffer as social group in civil, political, sexual and psychological spheres.
>
> — Considering women as object.

— The isolation, atomization and individualization of women's problems and consequently the lack of assertion of themselves.

— Not having to bow to male pressure to confirm to male stands, sexually, emotionally and intellectually, to be able to identify oneself as one feels is right and not to give into excessive demands for attention, time, support and all kinds of service if one feels one should not do so."[3]

The major factor of the debate, 'femininity vs. masculinity' is 'female sexuality'. Due to female sexuality, women are vulnerable to violence. It is the assertion that chastity as a value has been promoted by males in their interests. Since chastity is desired to ensure that children of a woman are born to the correct father, a number of restrictions are imposed on female, which is improper. All measures and restrictions are manifestation of violence against women, which curtails female sexual expression so that women will remain chastened faithful to their husbands. Another factor is the 'Feminine worth', which is the index of how a society values women, looks up to them with respect, and builds their self-esteem. Pandit Nehru once said: "We talk of revolutions—political and economic and yet the greatest revolution in a country is the one that affects the status and the living conditions of its women" (quoted by Usha Narayan, 1996). The UNO reports also says that women do two-third of the world's work, but earn just one-tenth and own just one-hundredth of the world's property. Usha Narayan also quotes Mahatma Gandhi: "Women is the companion of man, gifted with equal capacities, she has the right to participate in the minute details of the activities of man, and she has the right of freedom and liberty as he. She is entitled to a supreme place in her own place of activity as man is. By sheer force of vicious custom, even the most ignorant and worthless men have been enjoying superiority over women which they don't deserve and ought not to have."[4]

It is evident that a woman is not only different from men only biologically but also in several psychological fundamental attributes as intelligence, attitude and aptitudes. One of the many interesting differences is that females tend to see wholes, especially functional wholes, rather than the component parts which make them up. This is in contrast to males who usually tend to be able to isolate the component parts, therefore, they are more analytical minded. It seems that this gives the male some tremendous advantages, so that this difference and other feminine attributes tend to make female less good at various intellectual pursuits.

Like psychologists, psychoanalysts have also contributed to the study of feminine and masculine traits. Freud regards 'femininity' basically as a biological phenomenon and studies it in the light of the standards represented by masculinity. The absence of external genitals in a woman is a central factor in his analysis of feminine character which is primarily the outcome of a girl's discovery of her own 'castration'. "The feminine character traits are indirectly expressed, according to him, in feelings of inferiority, a sense of contempt for their own sex, of man's greater freedom and every kind of attempt to make up for biological deficiency among women which puts inherent limitations on their capacities. Freud thus claims women as weaker in their instincts than men."[5]

Jung, on the other hand, accepts the inner unity of the self, and interprets the feminine and the masculine as complementary phenomena. He calls the feminine archetype within man's collective unconscious 'anima' and the masculine archetype within a woman's 'animus'. He argues:

> "Just as the man is compensated by a feminine element (the anima), so woman is compensated by a masculine one...her unconscious has, so to speak a masculine imprint. This results in a considerable psychological difference between men and women."[6]

The later psychoanalysts Karen, Horney, Eric, Clara Thomson and others tend to depend more on sociological perspective in their attempt to distinguish the feminine from the masculine. Socio-cultural aspects gives us yet another angle to distinguish feminine from masculine. Most of the differences between the sexes do seem to be cultural in origin. Sociologists have attempted to study the position of women in different societies of the world in order to gain an idea about the 'feminine' characters in a particular context. They have come to the conclusion that the feminine character develops in a different manner from the 'masculine' because of the operation of social forces. For the study of sex differences, we may say that nature (biology) makes us 'male' or 'female'; the values and norms of the society in which we develop make us 'men' or 'women', and the interrelations of these factors with the other biological, sociological and spiritual components of experience make us the kinds of persons we become. No single factor explains the complex totality of any individual personality or of the human species. A sampling of anthropological data has helped the social scientists to judge what behavioural difference the biological male-female difference makes. Margaret Mead's *Male and Female* (New York: William Morrow and Company Inc. 1948) is a pioneering study in this area. The sociological approach to femininity depends on the correlationship between sex differences in abilities, temperament and motives and sex roles in society. Simone de Beauvoir says in chapter one of *The Second Sex*, "Males and females are two types of individuals which are differentiated within a species for the function of reproduction, they can be defined only correlatively" (35). She again says, "Nevertheless it will be said that if the body is not a thing, it is a situation, as viewed in the perspective. I am adopting that of Heidegger, Sartre and Merleau-Ponty: it is the instrument of our grasp upon the world, a limiting factor for our projects. Woman is weaker than man, she has less muscular strength, fewer red blood corpuscles, less lung capacity, she runs more slowly, can lift less heavy weights, can compete with man in hardly any sport; she cannot stand up to him in a fight. To all these weaknesses must be added the instability, the lack of control and the fragility already discussed: these are facts. Her grasp on the world is more restricted; she has less firmness and less steadiness available for projects that in general she is less capable of carrying out. In other words, her individual life is less rich than man's."[7] (p. 66)

"Woman can be defined by her consciousness of her own femininity no more satisfactorily than by saying that she is a female, for she acquires this consciousness under circumstances dependent upon the society of which she is a member."[8] (p. 80)

It is therefore, evident that the concept of femininity can well be understood on the basis of masculinity-femininity contrast in terms of biological, psychological, intellectual and socio-cultural factors. Because of these differences feminine experiences and feminine sensibility which constitute 'the feminine psyche' is different in nature from the psyche of male. The 'feminine' character which is determined by the nature of the feminine psyche is 'made up of certain instructive psychological traits as well as certain socially conditioned ones.' While presenting the psychoanalytic point of view Simone de Beauvoir further explains, "The fact is that from the male point of view—which is adopted by both male and female psychoanalysts—behaviour, involving alienation, is regarded as feminine, that in which the subject asserts his transcendence as virile. Donaldson, a historian of woman, remarked that the definitions: 'man' is a male human being, 'woman' is a female human being, have been asymmetrically distorted; and it is among the psychoanalysts in particular that man is defined as a human being and woman as a female—whenever she behaves as a human being and she is said to imitate the male[9] (p. 83).

One of the first radical feminists to insist that the roots of women's oppression are buried deep in patriarchy's sex/gender system was Kate Millett. In her *Sexual Politics* (1970) Millett argued that sex is political primarily because the male-female relationship is the paradigm for all power relationships. Millett looked forward to an androgynous future to an integration of separate masculine and feminine subculture. She insisted that this integration must proceed cautiously with an evaluation of the true human desirability of all masculine and feminine traits. Neither obedience, as it has been traditionally exhibited by women, for example, should not be unreflectively celebrated as a desirable female trait, nor is aggressiveness, as it has been traditionally exhibited by men, to be incorporated into the psyche of the androgynous person as a masculine trait. In contrast, it is not only possible to combine in one person the complementary qualities of strength and compassion; it is also desirable because both qualities are likely to help a person grow and live in community. However, we can view that all these things depend upon the socialisation of a person that determines the nature of human being. Many radical feminists see sexuality as the crucial issue in feminism because 'aggression and the need to dominate' form a routine part of what is accepted as normal male sexuality. Male violence against women is normalised and legitimized in sexual practices through the assumption that when it comes to sex, men are by nature aggressive and dominant, whereas women are by nature passive and submissive. Radical feminism rectifies this situation by offering woman an innate identity confronting this structure of male domination with female qualities equal to or essentialised into, maleness. For example, women are more peace-loving, soft-headed and irrational pacifists by nature. This is the politics of feminism. Women are essentially different from men and are their subordinated gendered position. In fact masculinity and femininity are today identities and complexes of behaviour in the process of reconstruction. Therefore, the need is to improve the position of women through local empowerment so that they can take their decisions within the social ranges. In this direction, the viewpoint of eco-feminists might help in completing the unfinished tasks of the enlightenment. We may conclude in the words of Simone De Beauvoir. She wrote in the introduction of her book *The Second Sex*:

> "The terms 'masculine' and 'feminine' are used symmetrically only as a matter of form, as on legal papers. In actuality the relations of two sexes is not quite like that of two electrical poles, for man represents both the positive and the neutral, as is indicated by the common use of man to designate human beings in general, whereas woman represents only the negative, defined by limiting criteria, without reciprocity".[10]

REFERENCES

1. Kate Millett, *Sexual Politics*, New York: Doubleday, 1970, 84.

2. Terman and Miles as quoted by Sunanda P. Chavan, *The Fair Voice*, New Delhi: Sterling Publishers Pvt. Ltd., 1986, 2.
3. Abha Awasthi (ed.) *Modernity, Feminism and Women Empowerment*, New Delhi: Rawat Publications, 2001, 35.
4. *Ibid.*, 272-273.
5. Quoted by Sunanda P. Chavan, *Fair Voice*, 3.
6. C.G. Jung, Aton translated by RFC Hull, New York: Panceon Bcores, 1959, 14.
7. Simone de Beauvoir, *The Second Sex* (trans), London: Vintage, 1997.
8. *Ibid.*, 83.
9. S.P. Chavan, *The Fair Voice,* New Delhi: Sterling Publishers Pvt. Ltd., 1986, 5.
10. Simone, 83.

19 Feminism in Indian Scenario

Most urban English-speaking Indians are familiar with the word 'Feminism', but their understanding of it remains vague and there is a general rejection of its relevance to the Indian context. Patriarchal-religious traditions of India and overt or covert conservative super-structures have kept it from becoming a widely apprehended phenomenon. There is still a tendency to perceive it as the result of 'moral corruption' of women imitating 'foreign' or 'western' trends, arising from their unrestrained freedom and leading to promiscuous sexual behaviour. A critical analysis of the Indian situation would make it apparent that the aims of 'Indian feminism' should lie in the spread of education, economic self-sufficiency, preservation of human rights and in the awareness of the desire for liberation from mythical and social values which constrain women as well as men: socially, psychically and physically. Such ideas of emancipation or in other words 'feminism' is tentatively prevalent only in the elitist masses who have had the privilege of education. To quote Judith Butler, a Western critic, for an Indian issue will not be out of place:

> "Do the exclusionary practices that ground feminist theory in a notion of 'women' as subject, paradoxically undercut feminist goals to extend its claims to representation?"[1]

In the Indian context 'representational feminism' is the need of the hour to liberate women from their enclosed space so that they can redefine their secular identity and realize their claims and rights. The ultimate goal of such representational politics is in the preservation of human rights or else, in the long run, such representational feminism could be self-defeating.

Simone de Beauvoir's *The Second Sex*, which has been regarded as the Bible of the feminist, may also be termed as 'Gita' for the Indian feminists. The question raised by her in the introduction of the book, long time back, is still relevant in the Indian scenario. I quote: "Enough ink has been spilled in quarrelling over feminism, and perhaps we should say no more about it. It is still talked about.... Are there women, really? Most assuredly the theory of the eternal feminine still has its adherents who will whisper in your ear...woman is losing her way, woman is lost: One wonders if women still exist, if they will always exist, whether or not it is desirable that they should, what place they occupy in this world, what their place should be, 'what has become of women?' was asked recently in an ephemeral magazine."[2]

But first we must ask: What is a woman? "'*Tota Mulier in Utero*' says one, 'woman is a womb': ... And yet we are told that femininity is in danger; we are exhorted to be women. It would appear, then, that every female human being is not necessarily a woman; to be so considered she must share in that mysterious and threatened reality known as femininity."[3]

Simone's further discussion about the women has universal significance. It is absolutely applicable on Indian woman in general. She says: "They are women in virtue of their anatomy and physiology. Throughout history they have always been subordinated to men, and hence their dependency is not the result of a historical event or a social change—it was not something that occurred.... they have gained only what men have been willing to grant, they have taken nothing, they have only received."[3]

Jaidev quotes, "A feminist novel for India is not a novel which a woman will write just because she is a woman and knows how to write. It will be written by one who has understood a woman both as a woman and as a person pressurized by all kinds of visible and invisible contexts, by one who is not carried away by fetishes but is mature enough."[4]

No doubt that the availability of the Western feminist theory should not lead us to its indiscriminate application because cultural contexts must be considered first. This is inevitable because we have a different history, different ethos, different forms of social stratification and patriarchal domination and if we need a feminism specific to our social situation, we also ought to develop, as K. Satchidanandan observes, "a feminist literary theory specific to our own creative and critical situation by which is not meant an unconsidered abandonment of shared patterns of reading and writing."[5]

Thus, Elaine Showalter's tripartite diachronic phases of the Western women's writing into the Feminine (consisting of a prolonged phase of imitation of the prevailing modes of the dominant tradition), Feminist (consisting of a phase of protest against these standards and values, including a demand for autonomy) and Female (consisting of a phase of self-discovery) cannot help us in totality because there is no such historical linearity in the evolution of the Indian female consciousness. Vrinda Nabar observes that the "Vastly different scenario in India encompasses contradictions of a kind undreamed of in mainstream (Western) feminist philosophy."[6]

Nabar lists factors such as caste, class, economic deprivation, sectarian fragmentedness, size and numbers, overpopulation, the growing power of fundamentalist forces, the sway of superstition, female foeticide, and above all, the essential nature of what is broadly termed as Hinduism, which combine to create a situation which defies any easy solution. The Western individualism may prove to be impractical in the Indian context because the collective unconscious still operates on the principles of faith and dogma.

In India, sexism is still a threat to women, who are exposed to murder, rape, torture and a variety of other crimes. Feminism is often political when women stake a claim to their rights and privileges. Sensitive women writers do not lose sight of their plight in our society, and feminist agenda is based on the principle of similarity and difference. Writing about women by women is a clarian call to feminine representation by gynocritics in India. Indian feminist, Chandra Talpade Mohanty seems to endorse 'the feminist osmosis thesis', that females are feminists by association and identification with the experiences which constitute us as females. But she introduces a proviso that the national/psychological commonality is mediated by history, therefore one should be open to the temporality of struggle which disrupts and challenges the logic of linearity.

With the rise of feminism in India in the seventies, the feminist literary critics came to believe that women had to create a literature of their own, in which the feminine sensibility could consider and confront the peculiarly feminine issues and experiences. It was essential to do so, because a large part of the feminine experience is out of the reach of the male psyche and, therefore, an authentic and sensitive portrayal of the conflicts and traumas, in all their nuances, ambiguities and contradictions, could be achieved only by women writers. Thus later part of seventies and the eighties saw a spurt in feminist writing which condenses in its pages the vivid rage of the exploited female against the 'male dominion' that characterizes both the Western and Eastern patriarchal cultures. Such works presented women as oppressed, exploited, tortured, cheated, angry, alienated and rebellious; (Protest) taking different forms mostly sexual promiscuity and lesbianism. But this towering rage against the patriarchal categories and male domination resulted in biased and distorted presentation of man in the fiction. In India, to study female psyche is an effort to liberate women from more structures that have marginalized them; it is also an attempt to reinterpret their status in the world. Feminist consciousness has certainly given a fresh ardour and excitement to literary studies.

A woman's experiences of life as a member of a gender biased society formulate her psyche. Feminist critics have attempted to understand how social restrictions influence lives of women and how it has affected their relationship to art and literature.

Modern India is today the scene of feminisms. Various movements regarding feminism grow every year, but so do the factions within it: feminist fiction and journals carry on bitter debates, a group of women writers is occupying the front seat. Men and women at conferences contradict each other's positions at top volume. But even then scenario is changing and efforts to change the position of common woman is becoming part of the basic structure of culture. Most of the people in general feel that Western thought is creating courage in the common Indian woman to voice her feeling and express her innermost desires. This position, the turn to 'feminite' as a challenge to male-centered thinking, has stirred up curiosity and set off resonances among feminists. Modern critical theories lay emphasis on psycho-analysis because gender differences are now based more on mental life than on anything else. Equality and liberation are the two words the Indian woman is well acquainted with but she is also aware of the reality of her life realizing the absence of easy solution or smooth exit, and yet refuses to escape meekly from the seemingly, bleak scenario. Even those women who are more fortunate insofar as class, race, wealth, education and opportunity are concerned, cannot come to terms with the idea of a male-dominated society while those women who are less fortunate are contented when their survival needs are met; yet behind the mask they are victims of loneliness and isolation. In both the cases women remain the weaker sex struggling to grapple with the conflicting situations. They fail in most cases to assert their individuality, to overcome the sense of loss in rebellion and to resolve the identity crisis. Nevertheless, the tortured Indian woman, as presented through various novels, stands a resilient creature prepared to endure and prevail with the help of her inner strength and integrity.

The post-independence travails expanding educational opportunities, economic aspirations, the fast crumbling of traditional norms and the impact of Western culture posit the urban Indian woman's consciousness in the spate of an awakening, a confrontation against a male-dominated, traditional society. The pattern of evolution of the images of women, from romantic idealization to realistic portraiture has caught a great deal of critical attention. The study of literary articulation of feminine experience has to be undertaken by the critics as an exploration of an individual's destiny in its bare, unbiased and real context. Women's own unconscious is shaped by patriarchy and has been shying from the artistic delineation of her own experiences as a woman.

Mostly Indians view feminism as an off-shoot of Western women liberation movement or Marxism and looked down on it as a sacrilege of tradition. India too needs feminism as a social and literary movement. It is essential for women's emancipation. At one end, women are successful in space research and technical projects and at the other end they are the targets of sexual exploitation and getting 'burnt' for the sake of dowry. It was felt that time has come for women to unite and strive towards a set goal where men and women enjoy equal status.

In fact the women's psyche and their problems in India are totally different from that of Black America or White America. The lower middle class, rural based women who contribute their labour for agriculture and industrial production, are illiterate and bound by superstition. They are not even aware of the extra burden which is put on them and they suffer willingly. The middle class face a different kind of problem. Their education and employment have not given them much relief and equal status. These women have to cope with the burden of domestic responsibilities as well as the demands of the career, i.e. double jeopardy of the upper class, a few of them are aristocrats and rest are the neo-rich and the first generation educated. They have leisure and money more than they can digest. The Indian feminism spans all these categories. Kamala Das, Anita Desai, Shashi Deshpande, Shobha Dé and a few more writers represent how Indian women writers are weaving feminism in their works. Shashi Deshpande said, "But to me feminism isn't a matter of theory; it is difficult to apply Kate Millett or Simone de Beauvoir or whosoever to the reality of our daily lives in India. And then there are such terrible misconceptions about feminism by people here. They often think it is about burning bras and walking out on your husband, children etc. I always try to make the point now about what feminism is not, and to say that we have to discover what it is in our own lives, our experiences. And I actually feel that a lot of women in India are feminists without realizing it."[7]

Deshpande, unlike hard-core feminists, does not agree that being a wife or mother is something that is unnecessarily imposed on a woman. According to her, "it's needed". She craves for a greater sense of balance, self-confessedly she feels trapped in the woman's world. The strong point about Deshpande's novels is her delineation of the women's inner world, her female psyche. In order to make the process of change smooth and really meaningful, woman writers have taken upon themselves this great task of their crusade against established traditions. No wonder, most of women writers have given expression to their feelings in the form of fiction only.

Malashree Lal in 'The Law of the Threshold', makes a study of the patriarchal forces which explore the Indian women's situation. She analyses three stages of Indian feminism, which moves from interior space to 'doorway poise' to 'exterior adjuncts'. Anita Desai's first two novels explore the story of interior space. While the 'interior space' of Indian women could be the fulfilling role of a mother, wife and daughter-in-law, the problem of woman's identity in the family and society becomes more complex in the following generations. One has to consider Anita Desai's novels in such a social context or in such a transitional stage of Indian feminism. As her novels deal with the middle and upper middle-class society, the complexities of the 'have not' section could be safely left out for considering the feminist issues in her writing. In Desai's vision "The Indian woman is always working towards an adjustment and compromise. Few Indian feminsits really contemplate total change. Working towards and adjustment through the traditional role is much less drastic much more Indian. I think Indian feminism is more practical than theoretical. It is expedient rather than ideological."[8]

One questions such ideas of 'adjustment' and 'compromise' as these traditional 'values' do not offer women any respite from their pain and from the injustice done to them. One also questions Desai's parochial vision of Western feminism. To consider Western feminism as a departure from traditionalism is a superficial observation. Probably, it is the Western radical feminism which Desai opposes and which is more theatrical than practical. The ultimate aim of any feminism is to do away with gender oppression, for a healthy community existence. Depending on the nature of complexities in a culture, the nature of the feminist struggle is different. Anita Desai has no such romantic vision of a Utopia to include heterogeneity of feminine desire. The psychic dimensions of gender oppression in the Indian context is too acute even to dream of a gender-free society or an accommodative paradise. Her women protagonists, unlike her contemporary woman writer Shashi Deshpande's women characters, are not feminists who challenge male authorities. Desai's novels explore the neurotic explosions due to sexual repression in women. Men are either rendered as sexless or gendered as 'feminized' beings. As a feminist critique, Anita Desai's novels seek to analyze how the category of women as the subject of feminism is produced and restrained by the power structures through which emancipation is sought. Shashi Deshpande defines the liberation in context of Indian feminism. She says, "Liberation does not mean casting of your humanity. Liberation never means doing without the family. No, no, not To me. Liberation does not mean leaving your marriage. We are human beings. Human beings are social animals and we need all these ties... My only thing about liberation is that you don't give into oppression and cruelty. Liberation means you refuse to be oppressed, you refuse to give up your individuality, you refuse to do things which go against your conscience. You realise the potential you have within you, you don't let other people tell you what to do. You know what you are worth. You know what is your value. You take that into account, and this is liberation. This does not mean doing away with all ties."[9]

Shashi Deshpande considers herself as a hard-core feminist but not a feminist writer. She said, "I am a feminist, I am a very staunch feminist in my personal life. A woman is also born like a man with lot of capabilities and potentials. She has every right to develop all that; she should not be oppressed just because she is a female. She has every right to live her life, to develop her qualities, to take her decision to be independent, and to take charge of her own destiny. So all these things to me are part of my being a feminist. You may want to live with a partner; it may not be a husband, you may want to have a child without having a marriage—all these things also are part of it. I don't deny that, but the important thing to me is that you (women) are incharge of your own destiny, but nobody should oppress you. Cruelty and oppression should not be there between the two genders. This is my idea of feminism. I am a feminist very much, and I strongly react against any kind of cruelty or oppression against women or any kind of denial of opportunities to women because they are women... But as a writer I'm not going to use my novels to carry the message of feminism. Then it becomes propaganda. If you call me a feminist writer, you are wronging me, because I see people as human beings."[10]

Deshpande's apparently contradictory remarks to her interviewers confirm her developing attitude towards feminism. She said to Geeta Gangadharan: "I am a feminist in the sense that, I think we need to have a world which we should recognise as a place for all of us human beings. I fully agree with Simone de Beauvoir that the fact that we are human, is much more important than our being men and women, I think that's my idea of feminism, when you deal with just my work, then take me as an individual writer and deal accordingly. Don't call it woman's writing or feminist writing. Today we have women writing about women, for women. These works are being published by women, criticized by women, read by women and studied in the women's studies departments and so on. I hate this 'women's lib' separating women's writing. It is just self-defeating."[11]

She says that her novels are not a man vs. woman issue at all. Being a woman herself, she sympathises with women, and admits that if others see something feminist in her writings, she has not consciously done that. The women's world is like that and she just mirrors the world. The interview given to Lakshmi Holmstrom throws significant light on her stance:

"I now have no doubts at all in saying that I am a feminist. In my own life, I mean. But not consciously, as a novelist. I must also say that my feminism has come to me very slowly, very gradually and mainly out of my own thinking and experiences and feelings. I started writing first and only then discovered my feminism. And it was much later that I actually read books about it."[11]

To Deshpande's mind, no amount of theorising will solve women's problems—specially in the Indian context.

Anita Desai's novels explore the issues of gender from the Indian socio-historical perspective. Desai's first three novels are a study of women's depression resulting from their inability to grapple with their family situations. Some of her novels deal with the issues related to women's education and their aspiration to obtain self-sufficiency and a meaningful existence. She writes about women in the urban middle class who has had the privilege of receiving education. But obtaining educational qualifications and degrees did not until recently impel women to create their space in the outer world and acquire self-sufficiency. The 'Bhadra-Mahila' cult continued to dominate the social consciousness even in the 1980s and 1990s. The repression had taken a psychic dimension and women continued to restrict themselves within the 'interior space' as that was more acceptable to the respectability of the middle-class household.

Anita Desai along with Shashi Deshpande and Shobha Dé is in the jocund company of Bharati Mukherjee, Rama Mehta, Geeta Mehta and a host of others like Nine Sibal, Anuradha Marwah and Namita Gokhale, caring to join the select band of feminists in India. Their contribution as feminist writers does not merely involve revalidating the French theories on the Western model. Each one of them has daringly and realistically portrayed the feminist issues in the post-independence Indian parameter. While studying these novelists one can get a complete but unprejudiced picture of what an Indian woman faces in a social set-up which is continuously struggling to maintain a relationship between the tradition and the modernity. These post-modern Indian women novelists indulge in exploring the feminine consciousness of the women characters, their evolution towards an awakening conscience and how eventually this leads to enrichment of their inner self in a male-dominated society. Self-introspection and self-discovery help the women characters to realize their veiled inner strength. That's why fiction by these women writers constitutes a major segment of the contemporary Indian writing in English. It provides insights, a wealth of understanding, a reservoir of meanings and a basis for discussion. The women novelists focus on women's issues. It is essential for them to do so, because a large part of the feminine experience is out of reach of the male psyche and therefore, an authentic and sensitive portrayal of the conflicts and traumas in all their nuances, ambiguities and contradictions could be achieved only by women writers. It is in fact the way Indian social milieu is becoming more intelligible and gender more comprehensible through recent studies on woman and their artistic presentations.

Shobha Dé is a modern novelist who is famous for portraying the sexual mania of the commercial world. In narration of incident she is very frank and straightforward. Like Anita Desai, she has the gift of exploring depths, the subdued portion of women psychology. Says Shobha Dé, "I did write with a great deal of empathy towards women. Without waving the feminist flag, I feel very strongly about the women's situation."

Dé is the author of twelve books. She also claims to be among the first to explore the world of the urban woman in India. Through her novels and essays, Dé has tried to shatter patriarchal hegemony. By choosing a nymphomaniac as the central character of her novel *Starry Nights* (1991), the sexo-feminist writer Shobha De has set a stir to the feminist literature in India, followed by *Strange Obsession* (1992), a novel about lesbian, which has further labelled her as lesbian feminist, thus challenging the phallocentric myth of writing as an 'erectile' and ejaculatory activity. Shobha Dé, a freelance Indian writer, shocks the very ethics and taboos of the society through her writings which make her able to stand with Simone dé Beauvoir, whose name itself symbolizes the very spirit of feminism. Judith Okely salutes Simone by conceiving her "as a mother or sister to the female reader with all the conflicting feelings of adulation or resentment which those relationships entail."[12]

Shobha Dé concentrates upon women of the upper middle class. Reading her novels introduces one to a very different kind of experience. Her characters are working women, socialites who are intrinsically attracted towards the world of glamour. Guided by the desire to earn quick money and also to get a place in the higher strata of society, they compromise with some unbecoming demands of society. The resultant neurosis and afflicted psyche is well depicted by Shobha Dé. In her novels she placed the women in their varied roles as daughter, sister, wife, mother and the career woman but their problems are different from the rural women as portrayed in the novels by other novelists. Shobha Dé succeeded in painting a picture of a very different sections of society. She is bold enough to illumine the real human condition, the way girls think, talk when they are alone about tabooed subjects etc. Her writings have always provoked reaction because of their realistic in-depth portrayal of life and her capacity to expose society but she defends herself by saying that it is important for her to present this glamorous vision of a rare world. According to her, woman in her books are definitely not doormats. They are not willing to be kicking around.

True to her belief, Shobha Dé merely introduces the readers to the inner lives of the elite women of Bombay. She shatters the myth that these economically independent women have a life full of happiness and contentment. On the contrary she probes the psyche of her women characters to reveal the trauma, insecurity and agony that lies beneath the gloss and glitter. The psychological problems of women are the same, so far as human relationship are concerned, whether they belong to the upper strata or the lower class of society, whether they are economically dependent or independent.

Bharati Mukherjee's novels are an engrossing study in the progression of women from feminine to female as stipulated by Elaine Showalter. Her women characters are sensitively portrayed and therefore, are best appreciated in their psychological depths. Her early novels have a touch of autobiography but gradually her themes widen and her strategies become more complex. Her women characters are docile creatures who believe in wrestling with their own problems rather than trying to dominate their male counterparts. Their attitude is not of negation or rejection, but rather of affirmation.

Critics such as Usha Tambe, Adele Kung, and P. Ramamoorthi have considered her works as a significant contribution to modern Indian feminist writing. Her feminism combines an awareness of classical Indian values derived from Sanskrit and Pali works with contemporary women's needs.

Such a view brings into contestation Deshpande's own position that she would like to be recognized as a writer without the qualifier 'women' or 'feminist', although in her works one may explore an underline gender—specific issues and the politics of negotiating stereotypes of gender and morality. P. Ramamoorthi points out; however much she may deny the influence of feminism in her novels, it is the core of her novels. "Her heroines speak of Virginia Woolf's 'A Room of One's Own' and Betty Friedan and it becomes quite obvious that the women she has created are feminists (even) if she is not one" (Singh (ed.), 1991, 115). Ramamoorthi refers to Western feminist icons in his analysis and assumes that these are the only icons available to a woman who also wants to express her feminist sensibility. This is in keeping with the popular misconceptions regarding feminism, even among urban sophisticates. But it is not clear in Deshpande's statements, whether she rejects white, western, liberal feminism, or all feminism(s). If she rejects the White, Western, liberal feminism, why do her characters speak of Virginia Woolf and Betty Friedan? (In *The Dark Holds No Terrors* and *Come Up and Be Dead*). If, on the other hand, she is trying to formulate in her writing, a new, culturally specific working definition of feminism applicable to Indian/Third World women, why does she go to such great lengths to disown the label 'feminist'?

Thus 'Feminism' in Indian scenario still poses many questions and queries before the readers and writers. We, as Indians, have already started talking about feminism, reacting against the suppressing forces and protesting against unjust patriarchal practices. In order to make the process of change smooth and really meaningful, women writers have taken upon themselves this great task of their crusade against established traditions. Scenario is changing, and it can be noticed; as efforts to change the position of common woman is becoming part of the basic structure of culture. The problems before Indian women are real, but Western feminism is not the solution for their problem. It is only a luxury for a microscopic minority of educated elite women. This small minority is completely divorced from the real interests of the majority of women steeped in poverty and lack of education in rural India. They are unemployed, superstitious and victims of different types of exploitation. The educated elite who as basking in the sunshine of plenty and pleasure are oblivious of these poor women's problems. Also it is the country's women who are making noises of gender-equality, 'sex-subordination' and subjugation. The Indian women are fully protected by laws; more than in any other country and they are better placed than women in the West. Now women have to wake up and look around and start doing things for themselves. Preaching the feminist philosophy will not solve their problems. The change must come from within.

REFERENCES

1. Judith Butler, *Gender Trouble*, 3-4.
2. Simone de Beauvoir, *The Second Sex*, New York: Penguin Books (first printed 1945) (trans, 1984), 13-15.
3. *Ibid.*
4. Jaidev, "Feminism and the Contemporary Hindu Novel" *Indian Literature* (ed.), Jaidev, Shimla, Indian Institute of Advanced Study, 1990, 63.
5. K. Satchidanandan, "The Laughing Medusa or the Raging Draupadi," *Indian Literature*, No. 157 (Sep.-Oct. 1993), 8.
6. Vrinda Nabar, *Caste as Woman*, Penguin India, 1995, 26.
7. Wasafiri, 17, 1993, quoted in A.N. Prasad, *Indian Women Novelists in English*, Vol. I, New Delhi: Sarup and Sons, 2003, 121.
8. Anita Desai, A Sense of Denial and a Sense of Order (Anita Desai interviewed by Lalita Pandit in Patrick Colm Hogan and Lalita Pandit) (ed.) *Literary India: Comparative Studies in Aesthetics*, London: Routledge, 1994, 168.
9. A.N. Prasad, *Indian Women Novelists in English*, Vol. I, New Delhi: Sarup and Sons, 2003, 90-91.
10. *Ibid.*, 97-98.
11. *The Hindustan Times Magazine*, 12th Feb. 1995, 3.
12. Judith Okely, Simone de Beauvoir, *A Re-reading*, London: Virago, 1986, 5.

20

Glimpses of Women in Regional-Indian Fiction

> "Sri S. Radhakrishnan observed that Indian Literature was one, though written in several regional languages. Literatures in the various Indian languages not only reflect a common culture and a uniquely Indian vision and way of life but even in regard to form and style they substantially attest to the common influence of Sanskrit and Prakrit literatures in the past and to that of Western literatures in the present. It should therefore come hardly as a surprise if the image of woman in regional literatures impressed us as largely pan-Indian with, of course, inevitable local touches and variations."[1]
>
> —K. Narasinha Murthy

Indian literature is not limited to literature written in English by Indians. Many Indian icons have written their literature in their regional languages. From R.N. Tagore (Bengali) to Jayanta Mahapatra (Oriya), all have enriched the Indian regional literature. The emerging New woman and her image in literature, especially fiction, is a product of the inevitable transformation taking place in our society; as the country marches ahead to cater with the rest of the world. This study presents a wide spectrum of images of woman in fiction of various Indian languages. Taken together, they present unity in diversity and unfold the story of Indian womanhood. The similarity of trends reinforces the idea that though written in various languages, these literatures show a similarity in thought and conditions of life in the women's world.

Women in Hindi Novels appeared during 30s and 40s defying the social and moral code and quite a few writers of the 80s and 90s have cast her and seen her in the traditional mould. The problem of representation of women in Hindi fiction has three dimensions: (a) larger assumptions and attitudes, (b) roles and relationships and (c) social conditions governing women. It was Prem Chand who for the first time gave to Hindi novel its compelling human interest and it is clear with his concern with the plight of prostitutes in *Seva Sadan* (1918), with widows in *Vardan* (1902) and *Pratigya* (1929), free love in *Ranga-bhumi* (1924), *Karmabhumi* (1932) and *Godan* (1936) and disintegration of the joint family system in *Premashram* (1918) and *Godan*. He stressed the squalid indignities heaped upon women while exposing the appearances of the so-called aristocracy and while his sympathies always lay with the humbler classes and with women, his tone was fundamentally conformist. In the post Prem Chand period many writers, under the influence of Freud, tried to explore the Indian female psyche. Woman is mainly seen as a self-sacrificing female. The mother is welcome when she can be a good substitute for a maid. She is expected to obey the sons and daughter-in-law and follow their dictates quietly. Mothers have lost their sovereignty but not necessarily their deep-rooted prejudices. In Pandeya Bechan Sharma Ugra's *Jeejji* (1955) Prabha is given all possible love and affection till her brother is born. Her stepmother marries her off to a widower who is addicted to wine and woman. It is significant that while Maya of Amrit Lal Nagar's *Amrit aur Vish* (1966) loves all her sons and daughters equally and cares as much for Karuna and Varuna as for Bhavani and Umesh. Lai Mami of Shivani's *Kalindi* (1991) breathes her last still waiting for her son who has settled abroad. In Surya Bala's *Agni Pankhi* (1984) the mother turns both an emotional and physical wrek because of the cruel treatment meted out to her by her brothers-in-law and their wives and also her son and daughter-in-law. In Shivani's *Do sakhiyan*, old mothers are dumped in the old people's house by their pragmatic children. The two mothers somehow manage to overcome their sentimental attachment to their children and become self-sufficient and retain their dignity. The dying mother in Krishna Sobti's *E Ladika* (1991) is also portrayed in all her dignity and glory. The new woman has placed a value on herself without attaching too great an importance to her son. If we don't any longer have the stern, spiteful and indolent mothers-in-law, we don't always have self-effacing and self-sacrificing mothers either. Mothers have also become worldly wise. In Ramesh Upadhyaya's *Hare Phool ki Khushboo* (1991) the mother sides with the daughter-in-law because the latter earns more than the son and is more organized. The change has come in the thinking and it has become an accepted pattern to expect the daughter, especially the eldest daughter, to take up a job and help settle her younger brothers and sisters. In Rajni Paniker's *Pahali Ladki* (1973) Ma says, when her husband has to give up his job, due to prolonged illness, that once her daughter completes her education, their life would change. And so Ranjana, their 'Pehli Ladki' works in an office for the sake of their family. Parents' self-indulgence and apathy, and young girl's ignorance seem to be responsible for the rise in the instance of unmarried mothers. Shashi Prabha Shastri's *Naven* (1974) presents the agony of an unmarried mother, Malti. Likewise, the problems of a divorced, working mother, are to a great extent highlighted in Mannu Bhandari's *Aapka Banti* (1970). The principal-mother decides to remarry, partly because she feels her son would be looked after better and grow more normally under the supervision of both the parents. Not all mothers however remarry for the sake of their children. In Kusum Ansal's *Rekhakriti* (1989), Vinny, the widowed mother of grown up Malavika, marries Pierre for purely sensual pleasure. She is a social climber. The irony is that Malavika seeks her uncle's permission for her mother's marriage to Pierre. An equally matter of fact relationship exists between mother and daughter in Raj Kamal Choudhury's *Tash ke Patton ka Shahar* (1986).

But Mrinal of *Tyagapatra* (1937) stays with the coal dealer and yet Jainendra considers her soul pure and applauds her satitva. Likewise Manjari of Ila Chandra Joshi's *Pret aur Chhaya* (1943) and Shanti of his *Sanyasi* (1941) live with strangers without getting married to them, yet the novelist rates their 'purity' and humanity very high. It breaks the earlier myth of Indian womanhood that if a married woman is not a faithful wife, she falls from grace. Now we have Shakuntala of Bhagwati Prasad Vajpeyi's *Pipasa* (1937) who loves her husband's friend, Kamalanayan and does not for a moment think her weakness a sin. Kunti of Vrindavan Lal Verma's *Achal Mera Koi* (1948) is attracted towards her husband's friend Achal. Jayanti and Kailash love each other in Ila Chandra Joshi's *Sanyasi*. This shows morality has undergone a great change. It was hitherto based on religion. A prostitute is to be pitied, not to be condemned. Society has to rehabilitate her if it wants to undo the wrongs it has done her for centuries. The shame complex of the earlier days has been replaced by an angry questioning of the social and moral codes. Sangeeta of Mridula Garg's *Anitaya* (1980) loves her prostitute mother and is herself an accomplished dancer like her. But she would not stop at that. She becomes a doctor and vows to take revenge on all men, to avenge her mother. She breaks away from the constraints of birth without ever denouncing her mother and emerges as a very strong personality. Birth will no longer decide her fate.

Bhagavati Charan Verma offers a new interpretation of virtue and sin in *Chitralekha* (1934). We indulge neither in sin nor in piety, we only do what we have to do. In *Ateet ke Chal-chitra*' (1948), Mahadevi Verma finds the limits of dignities imposed by a woman's own soul much more definitive than any social parameters of her virtue. The female psyche is changed as it is no longer imperative to marry the man you love or to love the man your marry. Pre-marital and extra-marital relations are still a cause for anxiety but not for supreme or outright condemnation. And then there is this a new image of our liberated women. Naseem of *Hare Phool ki Khushboo* has physical relations with many men, marriage is important to her only as a safety cover for a working woman. Her marriage is broken and she believes in free love. Pramila of Shubha Verma's *Katmangoor* (1989) is a society girl. Husband is only a convenience for her. Uttara is a mistress here, a polished woman. In Shubha's *Freelancer* (1981) Rosy projects a practical viewpoint, 'it is not at all necessary to marry the man you love. Romance disappears as soon as you marry someone'. She had loved Peter ever since her childhood but married Kripa Shanker for he could give her a better life. Today's new woman has shed her inhibitions and acquired a new candour about her sexual self. In Mridula Garg's *Uske Hisse ki Dhoop* (1975) and *Chittcobra* (1979) married women have an extra-marital relationship as part of the process of their growing up and exploring their own personality, and not because the husband in either case was a blackguard or a drunkard or cruel or deficient in character and libido.

It is significant that all these liberated women reject social conventions but view their deviations in the context of these very conventions. In Giriraj Kishore's *Teesari Satla* (1989) Dr. Rama Sharma is also economically independent yet her husband keeps bashing her for no reason. The image of the self-sacrificing *pativrata sati-savitri* mother and suffering wife has been revived here in the Hindi fiction.

Pramila Rajdan of *Katmangnoor* was offered by her father to his guru for some *tantrik* attainment. At the tender age of twelve she was driven to the evil path by none other than her father along with her sister Bela.

Shahana, the freelancer, receives lots of letters from readers trapped in illicit relations between brothers and sisters, between father-in-law and daughters-in-law, between mothers-in-law and sons-in-law, between stepmothers and stepsons. She has received five letters from a 19-year old girl—the daughter of a high official. Her father has been raping her even since she was nine. The girl suffered in silence lest her tuberculotic mother should die of shock. Shahane does not know what advice to give these people.

Instances of rape not involving blood relations are also on the increase. Today's victim of rape finds it possible, though not pleasant, to continue to live. Thus Vandana Singh alias Bonie in Raj Kamal Choudhary's *Tash ke Patton ka Shahar* turns a lesbian and hates the entire tribe of men because of an instance of rape in her teens. In Krishna Sobti's *Soorajmukhi Andheri*

(1972), Ratti becomes frigid because of a similar experience but does not end her life. Manu of Suryabala's *Subah ke Intazar Tak* (1980) is also a victim of rape.

In *Sweekar hai Mujhe*, Rita buys a farm, lives all by herself in the wild jungles, adopts six tribal orphans deaf, dumb and lame, and spends a lot of money and time on their treatment. This kind of woman as a social reformer was first visualized by Prem Chand whose Sakina in *Karmabhumi* collects loom-thread. The 'New Woman' cannot remain confined to her role as a housewife. Vismita of Manjul Bhagat's *Tirchhi Bauchha* (1984) bored with the monotony of household routine, symbolises a woman's need to establish her identity and her individuality. Nasira Sharma's Shalmali (1987) and Mahrukh seek equality in marriage and other relationships. They don't want to become manlike. They want to remain womanly and retain their feminity—yet theirs is the search for dignity and for equality. They have jobs, they have money and power. Nor are they interested in other men. They are educated women wishing to make their marriages work. We have image of tolerant women but they fight injustice. They may have their limitations but they try to tell the right from the wrong and strive for fullness of perception and being.

Women in Oriya and Assamese Fiction hold a significant place. The noble women from the pages of history (Meera, Laxmibai, Jaimati, Padmini) were influential in forming a certain image of women in the minds of male writers and their women characters reflected those virtues. In Assam almost everyone knew Bengali in ancient times and could read the novels of Sharat Chandra in the original language. The Assamese people translated them into Assamese and Sharat Chandra became one of the most favourite novelists in Assam. In his novels Sharat Chandra moulded his woman in all their different aspects of love, chastity, tenderness, loyalty, sacrifice and also in their darker shades of nature.

In Oriya literature Fakir Mohan Senapati painted Indian womanhood in true colurs, especially in his novel, *Samaanatha, Guntha* (1902). The portrait of exploitation and agony of peasant women that he has painted is unbelievable but true.

Sarita, the weaver, whose possessions were snatched away and who was murdered, is heart-rendering. Champ is the epitome of evil. She represents a certain class of women who, with their evil designs, destroy happy households. The author himself says, "In the life of Mangaraj, two rivers used to flow—one is turbulent and full with poisonous snakes and crocodiles, and even destroys its banks, and on the other hand, the second river is invisible, peaceful and pure. In the end, after the death of his wife, Mangaraj understood that this pure flow is no more. If you place a container of water and another one of wine in front of a drunkard, he will select the wine and preserve it with care. But in the end, he will realize that the wine is intoxicating and poisonous, while the water is the source of life itself."

Fakir Mohan was the first writer in Oriya who depicted the social problems of women from a psychological perspective. Oriya writer Gopinath Mohanty has written extensively in his novels about the oppression and exploitation of tribal women. But in general in Oriya literature men have not been so unjust in their treatment of woman and have allowed women a fair share, perhaps because Oriyas happened to be a marital race in history and had a highly developed sense of art and aesthetics. The writers after Fakir Mohan who stand out for their efforts to highlight various facts of woman's life and character are Kantakavi Laxmikanta, Godavarish Mohapatra, Kalindi Charan Panigrahi, Bhagabati Panigrahi, Sachi Routray and others. Writers like Gopinath Mohanty, Surendra Mohanty, Kanha Charan Mohanty have also portrayed their women characters with depth and sensitivity. They combined in them the poise and elegance of the olden days with the progressive social changes. Women characters of this period are more lifelike and practical, independent and self-asserting, torn by rapid change of values and the psychological stress associated with it. The women writers of present time, like Basant Kumari, Binapani Mohanty, Pratibha Roy, Yashodhara Mishra deal at large with the socio-psychological problems of women, with a deep sense of involvement in the present male dominated society and its callousness towards human values. Heroines of some of these women writes boldly protest and assert their right in the society with grace and dignity. The women characters struggle for a viable human identity in the context of rapid social change.

In the Assamese literature we find multifarious images of women from folklore to modern writing. In the most popular Bihu songs, we see a dominating image of woman, full of raw life, sexuality and vitality. The image of Assamese women merges with the fertility of soil, green fields overflowing with paddy and bountiful nature. The history of Assam is full of brave and daring women who fought and sacrificed their lives for the cause of the nation. It was Rajni Kanta Bordoli who resurrected some of these fascinating women characters in his novels. He improved upon the images of these courageous women and made them more clear and bright. Many of his novels have the background of Burmese invasions which took place from 1819 and 1824 and brought innumerable calamities to Assamese women. To Rajnikanta goes the credit of elevating the image and the status of women through his various novels. But he has also depicted the helpless state of women battered by society and circumstances. In *Miri Jiyari*, he has shown that the heroine, a tribal girl from the Miri tribe, becomes a victim of circumstances. A revolutionary image of queen Phuleshwari is presented in the novel *Kono Khed Nai* (1967) by Padma Barkotoky. Queen Phuleshwari of Assam rose from the status of a temple dancer to become the powerful queen of Ahom dynasty.

In the novels of Birendra Kumar Bhattacharya, the mental agony and trauma of a raped girl is brought out very forcefully by the author. In *Mritunjaya* for example, we come across Subhadra who was raped by the British soldiers. The brutal sexual assault shatters her completely. Her trauma, her dread of social stigma and the wound to her psyche is so deep and severe, that she rejects even the sympathetic and compassionate human contact and in the end, she commits suicide.

Homen Bargohain is one is the most powerful novelists of Assam today. It is unfortunate that his novels are not translated into English or any other Indian languages. Bargohain has depicted the life of an Assamese prostitute very frankly in his novel Subala (1968) which the readers read with horror mixed with sympathy.

The Assamese women writers tried hard to build up the true identity and image of woman in their writings especially after independence. They tried to analyse the psyche of the exploited women with interest and understanding. Nirupama Bargohain wrote her novel *Eparar Ghar*, *Siparar Ghar* (House On this Bank and On the Other Bank) (1979). In this novel the main heroine, Pateshwari, is a beautiful village belle. On the bank of river Pegladia, a Marwari boy promises love and marriage and makes her elope with him to a hotel in Guahati. There he abandons her. He had not revealed to her that he was already married. The helpless girl is saved by a hotel boy, Sabin. Unfortunately she had to become the mother of an illegitimate child. Sabin, who loves her genuinely, marries her. But again the employer and the master of Sabin has an evil eye on the girl and exploits her sexually. But Sabin remains helpless as he is a mere servant. Days pass. Three children are born to Pateshwari. Sabin dies of a disease. Helpless and completely broken, Pateshwari goes back to the village from where she had eloped with the Marwari boy. With great difficulty she raises her children. She keeps the eldest boy with a businessman, with the great hope that her son too would become a big merchant in future. Due to acute poverty, she has to send her young daughter to work as a domestic servant to her old master. Once when a group of social workers, which took land donations and distributed land to the landless, went to her village, Pateshwari developed a great hope that she would get a little piece of land. But she was pushed aside by the headman of the village and becomes a victim of village politics and favouritism. Her hopes of getting land are dashed completely. Now her only hope rests on her son. She expected him to be her support in her old age and remove all her miseries, wipe her tears and give her peace and happiness. With only this great hope, she waited with her two daughters and suffered untold miseries. And to add to these sufferings, her daughter who was working as a domestic servant, was sent back to her mother by her master as she had grown up and reached puberty. Pateshwari of *Nirupama* will even remain a symbol and a fine example of a female character, created by a woman.

Woman in Bengali Fiction exerts a regal dignity and a maternal compassion, which makes her the motivating force within a society or household. It is only rarely that a woman has felt the need for a feminists' struggle in Bengali literature. Bankim Chandra Chatterjee in his novel presents Prafulla, a poor lady, and converted her into the ravishingly beautiful dacoit-queen Devi Chaudhuri. She is an activist who wields justice and power with self-controlled detachment. She also introduces restraint and compassion into a male dominated society very effectively. Ashapurna Devi's heroines yearns for a fistful of sky from within the confines of the joint family and the veil, which obliterates her forehead. Feminism is not an intoxicant in her literature as the woman traditionally steps out of perspective boundaries. Woman is the epitome of vibrant Shakti.

The writer's world of Ashapurna Devi is not her own personal world. Rather, it is an extension of home worlds of all of us. Touched by her pen, all roles, all characters, come alive in front of us. Sometimes as a young daughter, sometimes as an adolescent girl and sometimes as a new bride; sometimes as a woman, as a loving woman in whose womb a new world is beginning, sometimes as an aunt and an ageing housewife or as a grandmother or as an old helpless woman watching the changes in the society, from a prison cell. She is known for her strong female characters. She was also called 'Kitchen writer'. In her trilogy Ashapurna touches on the contradictory expectations from women in contemporary Bengali society. At the same time, she explores the inner desires and aspirations of her women characters, unfettered by expectation of the men and families.

Mahasweta Devi, winner of the Padamshree and the Sahitya Academy award, is not professedly a feminist. In the Neanderthal darkness of the tribal forests where her novels are rooted, it is a struggle against the extinction of an entire species of the petty peasant: "Feminism is too unbane a world. Nor is there any fortress of male chauvinism to conquer. Men and women fight shoulder to shoulder, against a common foe: The Establishment." Mahasweta Devi's women are black, barbaric and beautiful-monolitic with the primeval purity of the blackstone and red soil, they spring from. There is a naked exteriority in this feminism struggle insofar as there is no separation between class-consciousness and gender-consciousness. These women symbolize power, abundance and motherhood. They are Durga, the divine avenges and Annapurna, the fertile mother goddess as one.[2] Mahasweta Devi's women emerge as sources of simple strength and indomitable rural courage to their men. Her novels abound in examples of simple rural courage by women. Her women are, 'The pure women' (Hardy). Pure in the true undiluted black blood of the racial homogeneity of tribal society. Her heroines do not discriminate between class-consciousness and gender-consciousness. They are feminist only insofar as the immediacy and elemental appeal of her female rebels far surpass those of her men. Often, in her fictional world, a tension exists between two worlds—the world of destitution and poverty where the woman is accepted in her elemental roles and that of upper class avarice and debauchery, where her beauty and image are exploited. There is a strong unity in the tribal society, which cancels out the conventional frontiers of feminism. It is only in the upper *echelons* of society, that a Kowasalya can degenerate into a political cliché, a Daupdi be raped, a Jahnavi sold piece by piece. Within the tribal society, a woman's honour remains inviolate.

The image of woman in Indian regional fiction differs not only in her realization of her individual dignity and sense of equality with man but also in her recognition of her physical as well as psychological needs. One could appreciate women's desire for the full integration of herself as presented in a celebrated *Kannada fiction* by Shivarama Karanth. In *Maimanagala Suliyulli*, Manjula the heroine is a cultured prostitute of the old traditional type. Karanth puts before us the three encounters of hers, only the third giving her total satisfaction, gratifying her body, mind and spirit, while the other two providing her only mental and spiritual pleasure or brutal bodily fulfilment. In an early novel of his, *Sarasammana*

Samadhi, Karanth offers a penetrating analysis of the frustrations of arranged marriages. If a Nagaveni suffers from a brutal first night, a Bhagirathi finds it intolerable to live in a house where a wife is treated as no better than footwear and put in her place. Another wife who attempts suicide is a sensitive educated young woman who finds her rich businessman husband a dreadful bore. He offers her no companionship, being out the whole day and feels the need for her for a few minutes at night. The questions asked in the novel are, in marriage husband and wife unite no doubt but what about their minds? Is woman only an object of sacrifice on the alter of man's lust, very much like a cock offered to a spirit?

The first novel in Kannada *Indira Bai* published in the last year of the last century, recounts the tribal life of a young widow and then describes how with the help of an enlightened family she educates herself and gets married to the son of that family; who after his higher education has become a civil servant. Kailasam's play (The Prostitute) presents the picture of a prostitute with a golden heart, who tries her best to ensure that her daughter will not have to suffer her fate and finally kills herself and her daughter when she senses that she will not succeed.

An interesting work in this connection is a modern interpretation of the character of Madhavi by a largely feminist writer, Anupama Niranjan. Her novel *Madhavi* delineates the circumstances in which princess Madhavi, daughter of King Yayati, is offered for a short period to a Brahmin disciple of sage Vishwamitra to enable him to pay his gurudakshina. She has then to suffer as being made over in succession to three separate kings to each of whom she bears a child and then finally offered to the Guru himself to meet this balance of the gurudakshina and after bearing the Guru also a child, she is restored to her father who arranges for her *swayamwara* in due course for giving her properly in marriage. Anupama's Madhavi protests against such exploitation of women and rejects the *swayamwara*.

Alongside of men writers show have written with great imaginative understanding of women, Kannada can boast of a long tradition of women writers who write, as it were, from inside. They have brought us a close understanding of women's thoughts and feelings, their attitudes and beliefs and of their individual personality and their place in society. Rightly K. Narasinha Murthy said, "The image of woman that emerges from the literature in Kannada, both ancient and modern, is an image at once of great dignity and dynamics, a combination of the virtues of a Sita and a Draupadi, now suitably updated."[3]

The two pioneering novelists of Malayalam, namely O Chandu Menon (1847-89) and C.V. Raman Pillai (1858-1922) have created some unforgettable women characters in their novels. *Indulekha* is a novel which presents a woman called Indulekha as the typical model of a progressive, English educated modern girl. Unconventional and revolutionary in outlook, she took her own decisions and boldly rejected the age-old custom of arranged marriage. She thought that she was free to select her own life partner. Of the many characters of C.V.'s novels, Subhadra and Parukuty stand head and shoulders above all others. Madhavi Kutti or Kamala Das as she is known, is the great feminist writer of the modern age. She even seems to go to the extent of justifying free sex for her women. According to her, it is not prostitution if a girl goes to bed with a man she really likes. The real prostitution is when one is forced to go to bed with a man one does not like, even if he is her own husband. Rajalakshmi explored the female psyche in her two novels *A Way* and *Some Shadows and Ego*.

Thus these pictures of Indian women presented by Indian authors in different Indian languages, prove that, for India, feminism is a reality. It exists everywhere; though in a different form and level. Indian womanhood is on the crossroads. More and more women writers are becoming iconoclasts. They are not satisfied with just 'Roti, Kapda and Makaan'. They want something more. The need of the hour is to explore the feminine psyche. To understand the female folk, their innermost desires, thought process and their individuality must be considered in the right spirit. Indian men, if they want to create a just society (of humans, of course), must weigh the importance of the fair sex. It should not be misunderstood that women should be given a higher place than men. The need is to remove the gender bias and to give them equal opportunities and equal rights to survive.

REFERENCES

1. K. Narasinha Murthy, "The Image of Women in Kannada Literature," an essay presented in the seminar, organized by N.M.K.R.V. College for Women, Bangalore.
2. Yashoda Bhat, *The Image of Women in Indian Literature*, B.R. Publishing Corporation, New Delhi, 1993, 67.
3. K. Narasinha Murthy, *Image of Women*, 16-17.

Bibliography

Abey, Mukta, and Vinay Kirpal, 1998, *Shashi Deshpande: A Feminist Study of Her Fiction*, Delhi, B.R. Publishing House.

Arora, Neena, *Nayantara Sahgal and Doris Lessing: A Feminist Study in Comparison*, New Delhi, Prestige Books, 1991.

Ashcraft, Bell et al., 1989, *The Empire Writes Back: Theory and Practice in Postcolonial Literatures*, London, Routledge.

Atwood, Margaret, *Surfacing*, New York, Popular Library, 1976.

Bai, K. Meera, "Feminism as an Extension of Existentialism: Women in Indian English Fiction." *The Commonwealth Review*, Vol. 6, No. 1, 1994-95.

Bande, Usha, *The Novels of Anita Desai*, New Delhi, Prestige, 1988.

Bartky, Sandra Lee, "Toward a Phenomenology of Feminist Consciousness." *Feminism and Philosophy*. Totow, N.J. Rowman and Littlefield, 1977.

Bhatnagar, Manmohan K., *Indian Writings in English*, Vol. 1, New Delhi, Atlantic Publishers and Distributors (P) Ltd., 2001.

Bordo, Susan, "Postmodern subject, postmodern bodies." *Feminist Studies* 18, 1, Spring, 1992.

Carden, Maren Lockwood, *The New Feminist Movement*, New York, Russell, Sage Foundations, 1974.

Chanchala, K. Naik, *Writing Difference: The Novels of Shashi Deshpande*, New Delhi, Pencraft International, 2005.

Chandra, Subhash, "Silent No More: A Study of That Long Silence." *Indian Women Novelists*, Set I, Vol. 5 (ed.) R.K. Dhawan, New Delhi, Prestige Books, 1991.

Cheriskramare and Paulae Treichler, *A Feminist Dictionary*, Boston, Pandese Press, 1985.

Cixous, Hélène and Catherine Clement, "The Newly Born Women." *Le Jeune Nee*. Paris, 1975. Trans Betsy Wing. Minneapolis, University of Minnesota Press, 1986.

Cott, Nancy F., "Comment on Karen's Defining Feminism: A Comparative Historical Approach." *Signs* 151, Autumn, 1989, 203-205.

De Beauvoir, Simone, *The Second Sex*, New York, Penguin Books, First Printed 1949, 1984 (trans).

De Graaf, Lawrence B., "Race, Sex and Penguin: Black Women in the American West, 1850-1920." *Pacific Historical Review*, 49, 2 (May 1980).

Derride, Jaques, *Eperous: de styles de Nietzche*, Paris, Flammareen, 11978. Trans. Barbara Harlow, Spurs, Nietzche's Styles, Chicago, University of Chicago Press, 1979.

Dhawan, R.K., *Indian Women Novelists*, Set I, Vol. 5, New Delhi, Prestige Books, 1991.

Donovan, Josephine, *Feminist Theory: The Intellectual Traditions of American Feminism*, New York, Fredrick Unger Publishing Co., 1985.

Drairie, Betsy, "Refusing the Wisdom of Soloman: Some Recent Feminist Literary Theory." *signs* 15, 1 (1989).

Dreitus, Claudia, "The Selling of a Feminist." *Radical Feminism*, ed. Anne Koedt et al., New York, Ouadrangle, 1973.

DuBois, Ellen Carol, "Comment on Karen Offen's Defining Feminism: A Comparative Historical Approach." *Signs* 15, 1, Autumn, 1989, 195-197.

Dwivedi, A.N., "The Hub of the Wheel: Some Recurrent Metaphore in Shashi Deshpande's Fiction." *Critical Practice*, Vol. 3, No. 1, 1996.

Eisentein, Hester, *Contemporary Feminist Thoughts*, London, Unwin Paperbacks, 1984.

Fatterly, Judith, *The Resisting Reader: A Feminist Approach to American Fiction*, Bloomington, Indiana University Press, 1978.

Firestone, Shulamin, ed., *Notes from the Second Year: Major Writings of the Radical Feminists*, New York, Bantam Books, 1970.

Firestone, Shulamin, *The Dialectic of Sex: The Case for Feminist Revolution*, New York, Bantam Books, 1970.

Flax, Jane, *Psychoanalysis, Feminism and Postmodernism in the Contemporary West*, Berkely, University of California Press, 1990.

Fredrick, Jameson, "Third World Literature in the Era of Multinational Capitalism." *Social Text*, 15 (Fall), 1986.

Friedan, Betty, *The Feminine Mystique*, New York, W.W. Norton, 1963.

Fuss, Diana, *Essentially Speaking: Feminism, Nature and Difference*, New York, Routledge, 1989.

Gilbert, Sandra M. and Susan Gubar, *No Man's Land: The Place of Woman Writer in Twentieth Century,* Vol. 1, New Haven, Yale University Press, 1988.

Gilbert, Sandra M. and Susan Gubar, *The Mad Woman in the Attic*, New Haven, Yale University Press, 1979.

Gokhale, Sridhar, et al., *Developing Your English*, Mumbai, Frank Brothers, 1998.

Green, Germaine, *The Female Eunuch*, New York, McGraw Hill, 1992.

Heilburn, Carolyn G. and Stimpson, "Theories of Feminist Criticism: Feminist Literary Criticism" *Explorations in Theory,* (ed.) Lexington, University Press of Kentucky, 1976.

Hooks, Bell, *Feminist Theory: From Margin to Centre*, Boston, Sound End Press, 1984.

Hooks, Bell, *Yearning: Race, Gender and Cultural Politics*, Boston, South End Press, 1990.

Horney, Karen, *Feminine Psychology*, New York, Norton, 1967.

Irigaray, Luce, *Speculum de l'autre femme*, Paris, Minuit, 1974.

Iyengar, K.R. Srinivas, *Indian Writings in English*, New Delhi, Sterling, 1963.

Jaidev, "Problematising Feminism: Feminism and Recent Fiction in English." (ed.) Sushila Singh, New Delhi, Prestige Books, 1991.

Jain, Jasbir, ed., *Creative Theory: Writers on Writing*, Delhi, Pencraft International, 2000.

Jardine, Alice and Paul Smith, eds., Men in Feminism, New York, Meshuen, 1987.

Jefferson, Ann and Dravid Robey, ed., *Modern Literary Theory*, London, B.T. Batsford Ltd., 1986.

Joshi P.G., *Shashi Deshpande's Fiction: A Study in Women Empowerment and Postcolonial Discourse*, New Delhi, Prestige, 2003.

Kaur, Amit, *Women Under the New Constitution*, Allahabad, Kitabistan, 1938.

King, Adete, "Feminist Criticism and Indian Women Writers." *The Bombay Literary Review*, 1 (1989), 42-49.

Krishnaswamy, Shantha, *The Woman in Indian Fiction in English*, New Delhi, Ashish, 1984.

Kristeva, Julia, "Women's Time", *Signs* 7, 1 (1981), 13-35.

Lacan, Jacques, *Ecnts*. Trans., Alan Sheridan, New York, W.W. Norton & Co., 1977.

Lerner, Gerda, "Placing Women in History: A 1975 Perspective." (ed.) Berenice, A. Carool, *Urbana*, 1976.

Lerner, Gerda, *The Majority Finds its Past: Placing Women in History*, New York, Oxford University Press, 1979.

Mill, John Stuart, *The Subjection of Women*, 12th Printing, Cambridge, The M.I.T. Press, 1989.

Millett, Kate, *Sexual Politics*, New York, Doubleday, 1970.

Mitchell, Juliet and Jacqueline Rose, *Feminine Sexuality*, Jaques Lacan and the Ecole Brendienne, New York, W.W. Norton and Co., 1982.

Mittapalli, Rajeshwar and Monti, Alessandro, *Post-Independence Indian-English Fiction*, New Delhi, Atlantic Publishers and Distributors (P) Ltd., 2001.

Mohanty, C.T., "Under Western Eyes: Feminist Scholarship and Colonial Discourses." *Third World Women and the Politics of Feminism,* (ed.) C.T. Mohanty, Indiana University Press, 1991.

Moi, Toril, "Feminism, Post-Modernism, and Style: Recent Feminist Criticism in the United States." *Cultural Critique* 9 (Spring 1988), 3-22.

Moi, Toril, *Sexual/Textual Politics: Feminist Literary Theory*, London, Methuen, 1985.

Moses, Claire Goldber, *French Feminism in the Nineteenth Century*, Albany, State University of New York, 1984.

Offen, Karen, "Defining Feminism: A Comparative Historical Approach." *Signs* 14, 1, (Autumn 1988), 119-157.

Paranjape, Markand, "Common Myths and Misconceptions about Indian English Literature." *New Quest*, No. 129, May-June, 134-44.

Pathak, R.S. (ed.), *The Fiction of Shashi Deshpande*, New Delhi, Pencraft International, 2005.

Raman, Meenakshi, Critical Perspectives in American Literature, New Delhi, Atlantic Publishers and Distributors (P) Ltd., 2005.

Ray, K. Mohit, *Studies in Women Writers in English*, New Delhi, Atlantic Publishers and Distributors (P) Ltd., 2005.

Ruddick, Sara, "Maternal Thinking." *Feminist Studies* 6, 2 (Summer 1980), 348.

Sharma, Siddhartha, *Shashi Deshpande's Novels: A Feminist Study*, New Delhi, Atlantic Publishers and Distributors (P) Ltd., 2005.

Showalter, Elaine, *A Literature of Their Own: British Women Novelist from Brontë to Lessing*, Princeton, Princeton University Press, 1977.

Showalter, Elaine, ed., *The New Feminist Criticism: Essays on Women Literature and Theory*, New York, Pantheon Books, 1985.

Showalter, Elaine, *Women's Liberation and Literature*, New York, Harcourt, 1971.

Shriwadkar, Meena, *Image of Woman in the Indo-Anglian Novel*, New Delhi, Sterling, 1979.

Singh, Sushila, Ed., *Feminism and Recent Fiction in English*, New Delhi, Prestige Books, 1991.

Singh, Sushila, *Feminism: Theory, Criticism, Analysis*, New Delhi, Pencraft International, 2004.

Spivak, Gayatri Chakravorty, *In Other Worlds: Essays in Cultural Politics*, New York, Methuen, 1987.

Tharu, Susie and K. Lalita, *Women Writing in India: 600 BC to the Present*, Vol. II, *The 20th Century*, Delhi, O.U.P., 1993.

The Encyclopedia Americana, Vol. 12, Danbury, Conn, Grotier, 1987.

Tutle, Lesa, *Encyclopedia of Feminism*, New York, Facts on File Publications, 1986.

Uma, Alladi, 'Woman and her Family, *Indian and Afro-American: A Literary Perspective*, New Delhi, Sterling, 1989.

Vijaysree, C. et al. (ed.), *Remapping Culture: Nobel Laureates in Literature* (1986-1997), New Delhi, Pencraft Interanational, 1998.

Wollstonecraft, Mary, *Vindication of the Rights of Woman*, Reprinted Penguin Classics, London, Penguin Books Ltd., 1985.

Woolf, Virginia, *A Room of One's Own*, Reprinted Harvest/HBJ edition, San Diego, Harcourt Brace, Jovanon, Publishers, 1989.